Discover Eden

Empowering Christian Women to Walk in Sexual Liberty

By Liz G Flaherty

Discover Eden: Empowering Christian Women to Walk in Sexual Liberty

First Edition ISBN-13: 978-1720702443 ISBN-10: 1720702446

Cover design by Sasha Timen www.alookdesign.com

Copyediting and Pagination by Christina Files www.christinafiles.com

Dedication

For my spiritual mother, Harriet.

For the years of modeling true godly femininity through long walks, lemon bars, afternoon scripture studies, hot water bottles on cold nights, much laughter, and many tears. This book is for you, Mom. I love you deeply.

Acknowledgments

First, the biggest thank you (times a million) to my British hunk-of-a-husband, Andy. My champion and my best friend. Thank you for all the hours you sacrificed helping me process this book while you were finishing your own PhD in Social Work. I know you could have easily used your extra time studying, or maybe training for the next World's Strongest Man competition, but you chose to pour into this project instead. You're my World's Strongest Man, honey. I love you.

Second, I'd like to thank my church community at Lakeshore Christian Fellowship for supporting me during the process of writing this book. Pastor Gil and Debbie, thank you for opening your hearts and your home to me as I launch out into new territory. Knowing that you love us brings such a sense of stability and peace. Also, many thanks to every man and woman at LCF who has prayed for me and supported my ministry. What a blessing to be part of such an awesome, spirit-filled community!

Third, a HUGE thank you to those of you who read though the first drafts of *Discover Eden* and gave me valuable feedback: Jackie, Jaynie, Reagan, Mary, Brittany, Pastor Jan, Lucy, Kristel, and Esther. Your unique perspectives helped in more ways than I can count. Thank you for taking time out of your busy lives to help. And a double portion thank you to Reagan for proofing and editing more than once! Your help was invaluable!

Last but not least, Sasha Timen, my graphic designer. My sista from anotha mista. Thank you for not only remaining flexible and patient with me during the design process, but also for being someone I could count on during both the fun and not-as-fun times. It's a huge blessing to work with one of my closest friends.

Endorsements

*I*n our day and age, in a culture that is so highly sexualized, it's powerful when a book comes along that brings hope, freedom, and practical tools to walk out God's design for sexuality. We are thankful for Liz and her honest and liberating voice in *Discover Eden*. We highly recommend you get a hold of this book as we believe its impact will be both personal and for the Church at large.

Eric and Candace Johnson
Senior Pastors at Bethel Church
Redding, California

*R*ead and Learn! Liz does an incredible job in *Discover Eden* wading through topics the church only whispers about. She shares about her own life journey while holding it up against current culture and then lines it all up with scripture. This book is a must read for any person looking for answers around sexuality and areas mostly avoided. She uses humor, which is an anesthetic for learning about these hard topics. I recommend this valuable resource to those seeking for knowledge and understanding around these behaviors and issues.

Danny and Sheri Silk
Loving on Purpose Ministries
Sacramento, California

In Discover Eden, Liz has combined personal experience with godly wisdom and insight to help us understand and deal with the highly political issues surrounding gender identity today. Liz Flaherty brings a powerful, God-centered message that is filled with truth, hope, and compassion. This is a must-read book for those who are struggling with their sexuality in any way, and for those who want to understand and help.

Barry and Lori Byrne
Founders of Nothing Hidden Ministries
Redding, California

While many Christian leaders and individuals remain sidelined over the awkward complexity of today's sexually misguided and confused culture, Liz once again leaps into the fray with scriptural insight, contextual clarity, and conversational humor. Whether you yourself struggle with issues of sexuality, or are simply wanting to be better equipped to join the cultural conversation, this book is well worth the read.

Pastor Gil and Debbie Dirmann
Lakeshore Christian Fellowship
Tega Cay, South Carolina

Sex, pornography, fantasies, masturbation, same sex attraction—WOW. If you had an emotional reaction to any of these terms, this book is for you. If you are struggling in any of these areas or if you want to know how to address any of these areas in a godly, compassionate, and healing way, this book is for you. If you are a married or single woman who wants to know healthy, wholesome ways to experience love, this book is for you. If you are a young woman who wants truth instead of hearing about sex from worldly sources, Liz Flaherty's tremendous understanding will protect and equip you in the love experiences the Father wants for all of us. God's people can perish for lack of knowledge, and in the church this clear knowledge has been almost non-existent. But not anymore. Get this book. It will carry you to a new level of compassion, health, and love in the most intimate areas of life.

John and Sandy Boneck
50+ Pastors MorningStar Ministries
Fort Mill, South Carolina

*L*iz does a great job in *Discover Eden* tackling subjects that the church rarely talks about. I believe her honesty, directness and scriptural integrity to be excellent. She spoke to matters that affect ALL of us in some way or another. I would highly recommend this read to all leadership of spiritual communities. This is a valuable tool to have as we interact with 21st Century people and lifestyles, especially for Jesus followers. We, in the Body of Christ, are not immune to these lures and need to be aware of how to break those entanglements of sin.

Pastor Jan Timen
Rivergate House of Prayer
Talent, Oregon

*S*cripture tells us that there is nothing new under the sun. The topics that Liz addresses in *Discover Eden* are not at all new, but they have been sadly ignored in most church settings. We can't remember the last time we heard a sermon focusing on women's struggles with sexual addiction, pornography, masturbation, and same-sex attraction. Liz, in an easy-to-read and sometimes humorous style, addresses the issues of sexual addiction and brokenness for both single and married women. Her insights are both biblically and scientifically based. We are confident that this book will offer hope and victory to many who have perhaps given up hope of finding freedom in these areas.

Charlie and Julie Harper
Senior Leaders at Bethel Church
Redding, California

*H*ere we have a churchgoing, married, Christian woman sharing bluntly about the modern day realities of human sexuality that few people in the church talk about. But even more shocking is how she reveals a new world of sexual freedom and bliss that most people don't know exists, all while holding to a traditional interpretation of Scripture. And, not once does she stoop to the old, tired motivators of shame, fear, or rote adherence to religion.

This woman is just bold enough to believe that God loves sex, and that He thinks we should, too. Listen to this highly vulnerable,yet enjoyable teaching of how it's possible to walk hand-in-hand with the God of creation, even in matters as intimate as our sexual behavior and identity. Other Christian sex books don't carry the invitation to experience the "more of God" in our sexuality; maybe they should.

I have walked alongside Liz for the last twenty years, as I have also walked out of my own sexual brokenness. I believe this book is a crucial, God-inspired tool that the Lord will use to walk this confused and hyper-sexualized generation back onto a road of life and health. Romans tells us that the creation is eagerly waiting "for the children of God to be revealed." This book will help many women play their crucial roles of helping liberate creation "from its bondage to decay" and bringing it "into the freedom and glory of the children of God."

Ken Williams
Pastor & Co-founder of Equipped To Love
Redding, California

Testimonial

My father recommended Liz to me. He had just read her first book, *The God of My Parents*, and saw parallels between her life experiences and my own. For this reason he suggested that I contact her to discuss the possibility of her mentoring me.

Although I was anxious and unsure at first, she really put me at ease with her professionalism and compassion. Her desire was to see my total freedom from the things that bound me. I had struggled for years off and on with drugs and pornography use, as well as suicidal thoughts and tendencies coupled with a long painful walk with depression. I battled all of this while attempting to live a sin-free, Christian life. I can't remember a time in my life when I didn't believe in God, but there were certainly times when I didn't like Him or want to talk to Him. There were definitely times when I wasn't living in the freedom Jesus had won for me and was instead living in massive oppression and hopelessness.

Liz spent two years walking through and unpacking my life with me. No problem was too large for her to see God's truth and hope in it. Her goal was to lead me to the Father in every circumstance, and she repeatedly spoke life into my situations. She challenged me to rise up to the life I was capable of, rather than linger in hopeless defeat.

In this time with Liz, I discovered two main reasons I remained in bondage. The first reason was that I had an incorrect view of God. I saw God as a judgmental father who had very little compassion for my failures and who felt a lot of frustration and irritation when I messed up. He was most definitely not a safe place for me to go, unless I was at my holiest and therefore worthy of his time and love. Then, and only then, might He bless me with His kind presence. When I had earned it. This was a total lie that kept me trapped in my own efforts to break free from sin.

Secondly, I experienced various traumas in my life that I really struggled with because I believed that God had failed me as a father and not protected me. That was a very hard path to navigate because it only contributed to the belief that God was unsafe and didn't really care about me. How could He possibly be an awesome, loving father if He would allow me to experience such pain? While I had started to make tentative steps toward working these issues out, I definitely needed help and support in the process.

It has not been easy to open myself up to God and learn to trust Him as a safe place and a friend, but I don't regret trusting Him in these new ways. He has shown me just how deeply He cares about me, and how deeply hurt He has been when I myself have struggled with my pain. The thing about God is that when you suffer, He is right there by your side, feeling it with you. Jesus really is the best example of this, and He said emphatically that when we see Him we have seen the Father. It was only through opening up and being totally honest with God about my pain and my anger toward Him that I was able to move forward, and wouldn't you know it—He was big enough to hear it. I found that He wasn't angry, and He met me at every place with love and compassion. The grace He showed me during that time was so sweet, and it's still just as sweet today.

I still struggle with my emotions, compulsions, and fear. I still get prodded every now and then with fleeting suicidal thoughts or urges to fall back on old thought patterns and vices: "You don't belong here, there is no place for you," and, "Hey, why don't you just numb out and escape with drugs?" or "How about watching some porn?" And I have to make the choice to take those thoughts captive. I have to choose not to believe them, and to fight them with God's truth about my life. My journey isn't one of immediate, total freedom, but one of climbing out of a pit into the light, followed by the daily decision to keep walking in that light. Daily I choose to continue going to God and being honest with my thoughts, desires, feelings, and fears and allowing Him to love on me in those places. For me, victory doesn't look like one giant moment, but an ongoing series of choices to see my worth and value and to be present and open to life regardless of what pain might come. To be brave and hopeful every day.

I have been blessed enough to gain a lifelong friend in Liz, and I'm so grateful to know her. I am so excited for the journey God is taking her on. You can depend on and believe what she speaks, because she has walked through everything she addresses in this book in her own life. She covers many difficult topics with refreshing honesty and even hilarity. Her openness brings something to the table that is greatly needed in the church today. Read this book with an open heart to hear God speak to you. He has a plan and a hope for every aspect of our lives, and that includes the area of sexual freedom.

"Mary"

Table of Contents

Introduction

*I*magine, if you will, you are sitting next to me on a small, comfy, chocolate-colored couch, surrounded by books and woodsy decor. One of those cat scratch trees is sitting to the left of you, and it's currently occupied by two fluffy, orange kitties. You're a little freaked out for a second because one of them doesn't have eyes… Then you realize she was adopted that way, and you go "Aw…" when the second kitty, who appears to be a carbon copy of the first (except with a few more eyes), licks her face.

Next, you notice a tray of store-bought cookies sitting before you on one of two tan TV trays. There is no coffee table; however, these elegant trays are clearly superior. Very high-class. The cookies are French macarons, and it's obvious that these are the finest macarons money can buy at SuperTarget. You are certain that I scored very high in the area of hospitality on my spiritual gifts test, for I have (hopefully) made you feel at home in my humble abode.

The reason for your visit is simple. You have questions about your sexuality and your identity in Christ, or maybe you care about someone who does. You're sitting on this worn-out couch (sorry about the cat hair, I must have missed a spot) because you want to hear from a woman who spent many years addressing her own sexual brokenness and identity issues, who now walks in a greater measure of freedom from what once bound her. You ask for my insight because I believe in a transformative relationship with Jesus that is alive with hope and power. You take a French macaron, remarking quietly to yourself that surely, this is God's Own Cookie. And after a few more, you begin to pour out your questions, stories, and experiences.

You cry.

I cry.

You laugh.

I choke on a cookie as I laugh.

This is what I'd like you to imagine as we head into *Discover Eden* together, because in my eyes there are few teaching and counseling tools more powerful than The Couch. Few things are more important than one-on-one time with someone who has faced what you're facing and come out the other side, whole and joyful. I might not be able to really speak with you one-on-one or share my macarons, but I'd like to invite you to relax and open yourself up as though I were.

Over the course of my thirty-nine years, I've sat on many couches, in many offices, in front of many leaders, sometimes prostrate on the floor crying only before God, in search of answers and relief in the areas I was bound sexually. I understand what it's like to see freedom in front of you but feel it slip through your fingers. I'm acutely aware of how it feels to stumble through life, trying your hardest just to keep things under control. There are times you feel strong, but the skeletons still rattle loudly in your closet. And, of course, sometimes they come spilling out at the most inopportune moments.

I'm a woman who did not understand the purpose of her sexuality for a good portion of her developmental years and into her twenties. Growing up as a pastor's kid I hid much of my exploration from my parents, as sex wasn't spoken about often in our home, and when it was, it was accompanied by a sense of hopelessness and shame. I wanted to honor my family, yet my desire for sexual expression and my need for intimacy led me down some very hard roads. My lack of knowledge and my search for answers about sex (using my own poor methods) opened the door to sleeping with men, using drugs, battling depression, identifying as a lesbian, and adopting a pattern of heavy pornography usage.

It was by God's grace that He continued to pursue me and bring others into my life that spoke truth in love. After many years of freedom, I now do the same for others. My husband and I both minister to men and women who deal with issues of identity and sexual brokenness. We both carry stories of extreme brokenness in which the Lord radically brought restoration to our lives, and our desire is to give away what was given to us, to sow the hope that God can restore all things. We are both walking examples that nothing is impossible with God if you are willing to allow Him to rebuild your life—as long as you never give up pursuing His heart, you will walk in freedom.

My prayer and declaration over anyone who comes in contact with *Discover Eden* is that you walk away with a greater understanding of God's design for your own sexuality and what it means to cultivate liberty in this day and age. My prayer is that you will avoid the pitfalls that I often fell into because of my emotional brokenness, low self-esteem, misunderstanding of God's Word, lack of community, and so on.

In the pages of this book, I cover areas of sexuality I wish someone had addressed in my life, especially when I was younger and first discovering my sexuality. I give information in a way that I wish someone had given it to me—direct, practical, non-sugar-coated, yet still a little humorous to make it feel more relatable.

Introduction

I prayerfully attempt to speak into these areas in which I was mis-informed, delusional, and extremely bound, along with discussing areas in which I've awakened to a great adventure of life beyond sexual brokenness. My heart is to give glory to the Lord for the liberty I found in my restored sexuality.

More specifically, my primary goal in writing this book is to address the three main issues I most often encounter when I minister to women: understanding the godly purpose of sexuality, understanding pornography, and understanding homosexuality. I've seen women shipwreck in their faith again and again because of lack of knowledge in these areas. I was one of those women. Many times I shipwrecked and had no hope.

If you're facing anything similar to what I'm about to share, it's so important to know that this book is not about shame or condemnation. You may experience *conviction* from the Holy Spirit while reading—and I pray you do—but any *condemnation* you experience is not from God. True conviction from the Lord brings hope and solutions; it shows you the way out of sin. Condemnation only acts to accuse you of your failings and offers you no hope of finding a way out. Through *Discover Eden* I only have a desire to see you free.

I'm very direct about what I believe are the biblical boundaries regarding sex. The manner in which I approach these subjects is not meant to oversimplify, diminish, or minimize anyone else's struggles, beliefs, or experiences. After speaking to many believers about sexuality, I've noticed a propensity to overanalyze things, which results in navel-gazing. This produces a hyperfocus on ourselves and our processes, instead of resulting in living a transformed life.

People often remain stuck in their growth process when they fall into the trap of trying to meticulously define and uncover every motive behind every emotion, desire, and so on. I will speak to these areas, but please remember that hyper focusing on them alone is not the key to your liberty. Ultimately, one man is the key to your liberty. Jesus Christ and His unfailing love for you is the power that frees you. The journey to sexual wholeness and freedom is more than just trying to satisfy internal motivations and achieve your goals; it's about developing a relationship with the One who knows you best.

The greatest test you have at your disposal to ensure that you're growing in Him is to examine whatever He highlights in your journey—whether it's a tool, a piece of information, or even a person—to see if it always points back to Him (see 1 John 4:1-3).

Talking about Taboo Subjects

One day, I was praying and expressing my concern to the Lord about the public conversation I was entering into through my writing and speaking opportunities. As bold as I am in my passion to educate, I was hesitant about some of the subject matter. "Shouldn't some of these topics be discussed more privately, like with family?" I asked Him. As I wrestled with the idea of talking openly about sex in a public Christian setting, the Lord kindly spoke to my heart. He explained to me that He wishes all families would have these conversations, but that many people don't have families who are open to such talks, nor do they understand how to discern truth in these areas. He reminded me that so much of the information we get from the media contradicts a biblical worldview. This contradictory, non-biblical worldview is very persuasive, to the point where many believers question if a Christian sexual ethic even exists.

The Lord emphasized to me that He desires to mature our churches into safe places where information is shared freely in order to help those who may not have a believing family to turn to or who weren't sent out into the world with accurate operating instructions. Until our church culture shifts, however, there will be a great need to counter the worldly cultural ethic that defines identity through sexual desires instead of through God's design.

With that said, part of changing church culture so that open conversations about sex are normal and destigmatized involves teaching the church about the liberty we have as beings created in the image of God. Our focus needs to be on creativity and liberty instead of just on the limitations and consequences of sexual sin. It needs to be on the solution of the gospel, not the "no's" we use to keep ourselves safe. Time and time again, our attempts to sexually self-police ourselves end in abject failure. When we aren't in a relationship with the Holy Spirit, the false fences we build wear out over time, inevitably breaking under the weight of our God-given sex drives, which long for satisfaction. True obedience stems from knowing a love that is beyond our control. This love inspires us to submit to a larger plan that has existed since the foundations of the world were built.

Two Components to True Liberty

In current church culture, the words "sexuality" and "liberty" are not usually synonymous. Ask any Christian woman who's spent any amount of time in the church what the word "sex" brings to mind. I'll wager that many women would list words such as "purity," "abstinence," "chastity," "waiting," and "duty" just to name a few. All these have their place in our vocabulary, but by themselves such words do a disservice to the big picture of sexuality that God has for us. If we want to be completely accurate, there are other words that need to be included in our Christian cultural definition of sexuality: "glorious," "exciting," "wonderful," "exotic," "passionate," "satisfying," "fulfilling," and "electric" all come to mind. When we fail to acknowledge the full wonder, awesomeness, and uniqueness of our sexual design, we fail to represent these important aspects of our

Creator. When limitations are all that we focus on, we lose a sense of wonder and awestruck amazement at how good the Lord has made us. But when we expand our vision beyond mere restrictions and focus on our purpose, then sexuality is no longer negative. It becomes the gift that it was intended to be.

I also understand that the term "sexual liberty" evokes other reactions from Christians. Some people may be reminded of the sexual revolution in the 1960's. *"Isn't sexual liberty the problem in our society today?"* some may ask. *"Women burnin' bras, men dressin' like women, everyone sleepin' with whoever they please?"*

That's not what we're talking about. From a biblical perspective, sexual liberty has everything to do with liberty *from* sin and nothing to do with bondage *to* it. Sexual liberty should be the mandate of every believer. To be sexually liberated means that your sexuality is submitted to the Lord, and you are operating in the freedom Christ paid for. You are liberated by the one and only liberator: Jesus.

There are two very important components to cultivating sexual liberty—and really any God-given liberty—in our lives. **Truth** (information) is one key and **Relationship** (with God and others) is the other. This book can supply you with information regarding sexuality, but although teaching and testimony are vital in building your faith and experiencing all God has for you, by no means are they a replacement for relationship. Take the information I offer you to help further build relationships with God and others.

Even if you don't *personally* struggle with sexual sin, I hope it can help you learn how to love others in a broader capacity. Information alone will leave you still longing for more because it does not satisfy. Information about God will leave you with a religious mindset and a rule list of "do's" and "don'ts." *Information plus relationship* will empower you to make wise choices, because you will be close to the One who desires anything and everything that benefits you. Truth will empower you to stop being a victim of sin. Trust that you don't know all things and need to expand your vision, especially when it pertains to something so important as sexuality.

At first, I began writing this book with a specific age range in mind, but the more I prayed about it the more I realized that really anyone who's reached sexual maturity can benefit from it, even young girls. Mothers, you know your children best, but I would hazard a guess that they're having conversations about sex with peers and are being exposed to information about sex long before they're even twelve years old. If your daughter is one of the countless girls with access to a great number of Internet-enabled devices, I highly recommend this book as one of your resources.

At the same time, I also encounter many women in their forties and fifties who are in great need of knowledge and insight regarding their sexuality. For this reason, I've realized the audience of women I'm writing to is indeed very broad.

So why did I choose to write *Discover Eden* for all women and not split it into separate books for teens and adults, or for single and married women? I believe it's extremely beneficial to speak openly about sexuality to a broad audience of women for two main reasons: it builds connections between all women by encouraging empathy for each other, and *shared* biblical knowledge shifts a culture for the better. Tiptoeing around the topic of sexuality or being passive in sharing information has led to generations of people who remain bound by sin and uneducated about the gift of what God created. Learning together opens the door to understanding where others may be coming from in their walk with the Lord.

Even though I do my best to present broad information that everyone will be able to apply to their lives, there are times I address married and single women in separate ways. I encourage you to read the whole thing so that it fills in any gaps or challenges any misunderstandings you may have regarding sexuality. If you are single and desiring to be married, I pray this information will be educational and inspiring for your future. If you don't desire to marry, and feel there is a grace on your life to serve the Lord by staying celibate, then I suggest reading it all so that you can bring strength to others. And if you're married and are struggling with your thoughts or actions, I pray that this information helps lead you to liberation. Ultimately, we're all part of a church family, and knowledge is helpful to all of us because we are interconnected.

If you take offense to the idea of addressing the subject of sex in a very direct manner and with a hefty dose of humor, then I suspect you may throw this book across the room a few times throughout your reading. That's okay. Just keep picking it up. I pray that even if you're one of those people, you find yourself experiencing freedom in new ways.

I'm certainly aware of the fact that many of you have stories of abuse or neglect in your own lives and that any mention of sex can be difficult. This book does not cover sexual abuse, but I do feel that it can help aid in an understanding of what the Lord would like to restore in your life, whether that's the freedom to enjoy the gift of sex and physical intimacy with your husband or any other aspects of mental freedom the Lord has for you.

Being able to laugh and talk about a subject that previously brought much pain is a great big slap in the enemy's face for what he tried to sow in your life. Know that you are meant for joy and peace. You were created to embrace and enjoy all of God's gifts.

Now then, please have a seat and grab a cookie...or ten. Here on this Couch we're going to embrace change, we're going to fight for victory, and above everything we're going to be transparent. Because whatever your struggle may be, you were meant for more than this. Do not settle. Daughters don't settle.

Freedom.

Laughter.

Liberty.

Beautiful, God-given, firm-on-the-outside, soft-on-the-inside macaron cookies.

These are a few of my favorite things.

Let's get started.

Chapter One

The Garden

"We all long for Eden, and we are constantly glimpsing it: our whole nature at its best and least corrupted, its gentlest and most human, is still soaked with the sense of exile."

—J.R.R. Tolkien

The Origins of Sex

No matter who you are, understanding sex and the role it plays in our lives is crucial. When you have a limited or skewed understanding of sex, it limits your understanding of God: who He is, the nature of His relationship with the church, how we were designed by Him, and how He called us to relate to our husbands. If you are currently single and desire to be married, then understanding how God designed sex will prepare you for marriage and equip you for walking through healthy celibacy until marriage. For those of you who are married, rightly understanding sex will enable you to walk through a healthy and satisfying marriage. And lastly, if you are called to long-term celibacy—the type Paul talks about in First Corinthians—then understanding God's design for sex is important for ensuring success.

Before we continue, repeat after me: *Everyone needs to be educated about God's design for sexuality, regardless of their calling.*

Now let's get to it. In order to move ahead though, first we need to go back—*way* back—to the very beginning so that we can get a more complete biblical perspective of God's design for sexuality.

Adam and Eve: The Original Sexy Celebrities

The creation story in Genesis is the beginning and foundation of our understanding of the role of sex, sexual intimacy, and gender compatibility. Adam and Eve were created and blessed in the very beginning of God's design for humanity. God created man and woman so that they would not be alone. God made Earth a wild and luscious planet, then gave Adam and Eve the responsibility of stewarding all that He made in the garden of Eden. God designed humankind not only to commune with Him, but also to commune with creation. They were free to enjoy it all.

Imagine living on a clean planet, free of thorns, pollution, and cellulite. There were no bras, either. Eve was free from underwire and restrictive clothes in this blessed land. Also, nothing sagged, wrinkled, or ached, *even when bending over to pick something up!* Adam and Eve were truly free as free can be, in every sense of the word! No insecurity or jealousy. No wondering if their bodies measured up or if they were attractive enough for each other. Complete security in God's love for them and their love for each other was their everyday experience, and their bodies were designed and dedicated to pleasuring each other in every way.

It's important to note that as God created Adam and Eve to care for this paradise, this caring did not involve strenuous work. There was no backbreaking labor or fear of limited provisions—only the discovery and enjoyment of all God had given them. Continual paradise, enjoying each other's bodies, not working a single moment of the day, living off the land without a care in the world. They were the original hippies. The only thing missing was a Volkswagen bus with shag carpet and God eating a kale wrap in the front seat.

They lived in Eden. Eden was a magnificent work of art, set in place by a loving father. It provided Adam and Eve with all they could ask for. It was a utopia of foods, fun, and relationship with Him—a honeymoon retreat on steroids.

> *Then God blessed them, and God said to them, "Be fruitful and multiply; fill the earth and subdue it; have dominion over the fish of the sea, over the birds of the air, and over every living thing that moves on the earth." Therefore a man shall leave his father and mother and be joined to his wife, and they shall become one flesh.* (Genesis 1:28; 2:24 NKJV)

Sex in the Garden was an extension of God's gift of creation, meant to function as a bond between Adam and Eve and reflect the nature of God's image *in* Adam and Eve. His abundance in this paradise was also part of a mission to expand the boundaries of the Garden; it was a means of creating life, of multiplying humanity so that it could rule the Earth. Sex was just like the Garden itself; a thing of both function and pleasure, of both creation and beauty, and as such it was key in growing Eden's borders. It would bring children, form new family units, spread the beauty of God's creation further and further out into the world. And one important thing about sex is that it also created a strong unity between males and females. No matter how far the Garden spread or how many of God's children ate of its fruit, there would always exist a unique relationship between man and woman, mother and father. Even on top of being pleasurable and productive, sex brought man and woman together and strengthened their love for each other.

So, the garden of Eden expanded and Adam and Eve enjoyed paradise without any awareness of evil or pain. As such, there was no need for clothes, sunblock, guns, or bug repellent. They simply had no knowledge of such things, because they had only been exposed to God and His never-ending goodness.

Evil did exist, however, outside of the Garden. I imagine Eden expanding out into the emptiness of the Earth, displacing the evil there. There was no locked gate around Eden, so in this expanding paradise there was one boundary the Lord put in place for Adam and Eve's protection: *"...but you must not eat from the Tree of the Knowledge of Good and Evil, for when you eat from it you will certainly die"* (Genesis 2:17 NIV). If they stayed away from that tree and never ate its fruit, all would be well. And before He set that boundary, death wasn't even an aspect of their lives. They only knew eternity; their bodies were immortal because they were made to reflect the image of God, and God is immortal.

It's important to note that the Bible's use of "death" here did not mean that they would physically die right then and there if they ate from the tree. This death, according to the Bible, meant a separation from God. This spiritual death would lead to a physical death, even though God intended both spiritual and physical life to be eternal. It would mean the end of hippie paradise because it would mean they had chosen another love and lord over Him.

God wanted His children to live in complete freedom, so even then, at the beginning of time, He gave them the power of free choice. They could live in their hippie paradise, or they could live in darkness.

The Tree of the Knowledge of Good and Evil wasn't the only noteworthy tree in the Garden, though. There was also the Tree of

Life, and eating of its fruit would allow them to
right, not only were they free to eat, have sex,
God all they wanted, but they could do it with
or dying. As long as they kept away from the one to ͝
stayed within Eden's borders, this hippie honeymoon party pa͝
would last forever. And believe it or not, this level of abundance,
safety, and intimacy was God's will for all of humanity.

But, tragically, this honeymoon would come to an abrupt end.

The Fall of Paradise

It wasn't long before Satan entered the picture. But who is Satan? I've heard a surprising amount of misinformation regarding Satan and his origins, mostly thanks to his portrayal in fictional media. Some falsely believe he's some sort of equal to God, an entity in an eternal duel with the Creator. In reality, Satan was originally part of God's perfect creation. Satan was a cherub, a heavenly being, the highest of all angels, created by God with the ability to choose his own destiny. Satan was beautiful and full of ability; his function was to bring glory and worship to God.

Instead of bringing God praise, however, he let his own selfish desires destroy him. Instead of praising God, Satan desired most to be God. And because of this desire to take the throne of heaven, God kicked him out. Because of his arrogance and pride, God took away his authority, so Satan roamed the Earth, disconnected from God and the rest of the heavenly host.

Satan's identity became one of lies and deception. The Bible calls him the author of lies (see John 8:44). God, on the other hand, simply cannot lie, because God is perfect love. And since Satan is a liar and hates anything created by God, naturally his first plan of action on Earth was to steal from humanity.

The Garden

No evil beings were allowed to enter the garden of Eden though, so Satan needed to take another form. He settled on something safe and familiar so that he could more effectively twist the truth, something that Adam and Eve had dominion over: an animal. He chose a snake.

And while you or I might have a few problems with a snake just cruising on up to us when we're sitting under a tree, munching on some mango—especially if it started to talk to us—Adam and Eve had no fear of animals. The Bible doesn't say anything about Eve being scared or confused when Satan approached her.

Now the serpent was more crafty than any other beast of the field that the Lord God had made. He said to the woman, "Did God actually say, 'You shall not eat of any tree in the garden?'" And the woman said to the serpent, "We may eat of the fruit of the trees in the garden, but God said, 'You shall not eat of the fruit of the tree that is in the midst of the garden, neither shall you touch it, lest you die.'" But the serpent said to the woman, "You will not surely die. For God knows that when you eat of it your eyes will be opened, and you will be like God, knowing good and evil." So when the woman saw that the tree was good for food, and that it was a delight to the eyes, and that the tree was to be desired to make one wise, she took of its fruit and ate, and she also gave some to her husband who was with her, and he ate. Then the eyes of both were opened, and they knew that they were naked. And they sewed fig leaves together and made themselves loincloths.

And they heard the sound of the Lord God walking in the garden in the cool of the day, and the man and his wife hid themselves from the presence of the Lord God among the trees of the garden. But the Lord God called to the man and said to him, "Where are you?" And he said, "I heard the sound of you in the garden, and I was afraid, because I was naked, and I hid myself." He said, "Who told you that you were naked? Have you eaten of the tree of which I commanded you not to eat?" The man said, "The woman whom you gave to be with me, she gave me fruit of the tree, and I ate." Then the Lord God said to the woman, "What is this that you have done?" The woman said, "The serpent deceived me, and I ate." (Genesis 3:1-13 ESV)

Satan's Access to Authority

Eve's own selfish desires to obtain wisdom opened the door to her deception. Satan didn't take over Eve's body and force her to eat. Satan merely tricked Eve into doing so. He deceived her into thinking that God was withholding from her. He twisted something God said and convinced Eve that God's boundaries were to keep her and Adam from the powerful experience of "knowing," when really these boundaries were for their own protection against evil. God was *never* interested—and is *still* not interested, I might add—in withholding any good thing.

But Eve traded her identity as a daughter who trusted her father for one of an orphan who distrusted her caregiver. Her actions ushered into the world the lies that God is manipulative instead of protective and that He wants to limit us. Eve and Adam went from obeying God to obeying Satan. They handed over their God-given mission to a being that hated them and, instead of living as a son and daughter, they became slaves.

This act of mistrust introduced humanity to sin and death. God stripped away their paradise, their authority, and their access to the Tree of Life. God sent them from Eden out into the world with the new knowledge that evil existed, and their sin introduced all manner of strenuous work into their lives. It introduced pain, suffering, fear, and ultimately death.

Their relationship with God was broken and even their relationship with each other was burdened by Satan's distortion. Satan now had the opportunity to rule over the Earth, taking every chance possible to perpetuate lies about God and destroy His creation.

It may seem like cruelty on God's part, considering this was a first offense. In reality, however, this was God's way of giving His creation the gift of free will. If God wished, He could have let Adam and Eve remain in the Garden and allowed them to continue eating from the Tree of Life...but if He did that, His children would live under this curse forever. By sending them away from the Garden, God was giving them the only option that would someday lead them to freedom from the curse. Despite all this new trouble sin brought into the world, He had a plan, because He is an all-loving and all-redemptive God.

We Could Use a Savior Right About Now

In order to break the curse and restore us to our rightful places as sons and daughters of the Creator, God sent His own Son down to Earth. This Son was the second Adam, our new Tree of Life, Jesus Christ. Jesus was obedient and perfect in every way because He *was* God, sent to us in a humble form, and He died to fulfill the law and give us back the authority we lost in the Garden. In doing this, He restored our close and communal relationship with God. Through believing that Jesus is who He says He is—the Savior of the world—we are restored to where we were in the Garden.

We still live in a world where there is pain and toil, and we're not literally back in Eden itself, but the curse of disconnection has been broken. Jesus' death and resurrection breaks all curses, even those we experience today. In fact, I'd say things are actually *better* today than they were in the Garden. God doesn't physically walk with us, and this sure ain't no 24/7 hippie love fest, but His spirit now lives *within us*. That's something Adam and Eve did not have.

And there's more to this than just our own restoration. Jesus also came to demonstrate how to expand the power of the kingdom of God once again. He taught us that salvation was just the beginning of our role as believers. Back in our rightful place as sons and daughters of God, we're tasked with more than just happily continuing along with our lives; He has also tasked us with expanding the garden (His kingdom) and destroying the powers of darkness. Even better, we now have the Holy Spirit to guide us out of all bondage to sin and to help us on our journey through this fallen and decaying world.

Jesus gave us a new mandate in Matthew 28:18-20 (NIV):

Then Jesus came to them and said, "All authority in heaven and on Earth has been given to me. Therefore, go and make disciples of all nations, baptizing them in the name of the Father and of the Son and of the Holy Spirit, and teaching them to obey everything I have commanded you. And surely, I am with you always, to the very end of the age."

Our mission now is to drive out the powers of darkness by walking in our God-given authority. We are called to expand the kingdom of God by bringing heaven to Earth as Jesus prayed in Matthew 6:10: *"Your kingdom come. Your will be done. On earth as it is in heaven"* (ESV). This means breaking free from everything that holds our identities in Christ captive, then declaring the good news to others.

Chapter Two

God's Design for Sex

"The heart is God's most magnificent creation, and the prize over which He fights the kingdom of darkness. Now consider this— marriage is the sanctuary of the heart. You have been entrusted with the heart of another human being. Whatever else your life's great mission will entail, loving and defending this heart next to you is part of your great quest."

—John Eldridge

Marriage

What do fruit trees, cosmic battles, and Jesus have to do with sex in this modern day and age? What is sex's purpose, other than a natural physical expression between two people? Where is the harm in sex outside of marriage? Isn't sex within marriage an outdated concept? Well, I'm so glad you asked.

The Bible teaches us that marriage is not just a human institution (a legal partnership for the purposes of ownership and taxes and whatnot), but that it's also *divine*. This means that God defined the role of marriage and that we should honor it. And like any other principle established by God, when we honor it, we live in harmony with His will. In fact, I would say that the covenant of marriage is one of the most important godly principles to understand, and since it's described in detail throughout the Old and New Testaments, it's logical to conclude that God meant for us to value biblical marriage today.

First, let's begin by looking at what a covenant is and why God uses this word to define marriage. A covenant is a mutual relationship in which two parties promise something to each other. Within a godly covenant, both people willingly enter into an agreement, and it's important to understand that they're both choosing what they bring to the table.

God intends the covenant of marriage to involve two empowered people willingly committing to each other for a lifetime—not two coerced or overpowered people becoming slaves to one another. The Bible always describes marriage as being between a man and a woman who commit not only their hearts to each other but their bodies and minds as well. God's will is to bless those two people so that they can live in unity and love for the rest of their lives. In Ephesians 5:25-30, marriage is described as mutual and overflowing with loving acts.

It's also a public agreement made before other people and God Himself, and it's meant to be permanent. "Until death do us part" is a phrase we often hear at traditional weddings, and this comes from the idea that death is ultimately the only thing that breaks that sacred agreement. There are certain circumstances in which the terms of the covenant are violated, resulting in divorce, but otherwise marriage isn't easily tossed away—it's for life.

It's also meant to be exclusive, which means that no matter what, the covenant will not extend to include other people. God made it exclusive as a way to safeguard our bodies and souls, because it's the single most intimate kind of relationship two people can have with each other. That's why Jesus makes it clear in Matthew 5:28 that even lusting after another person in your mind is considered straying from the boundaries of marriage. Paul also talks a lot about marriage in the New Testament.

For we are members of His body, of His flesh and of His bones. For this reason, a man shall leave his father and mother and be joined to his wife, and the two shall become one flesh. This is a great mystery, but I speak concerning Christ and the Church. (Ephesians 5:30-32 NKJV)

Paul describes marriage as being a mirror image of the relationship that Christ has with the church (which is us). In Christ, we become one body, just as a husband and wife become one flesh, and ultimately this points us back to God's origins of sex in the Garden. Jesus is the perfect picture of a sacrificial God who laid down His life, even suffering a horrific death, because of His great love for the church. It may seem way too amazing, too good to be true, but this is the example the New Testament sets for our marriages.

Sex (And Why It Belongs in Marriage)

Sex is the outward sign of the divine covenant. It's the physical act that reminds us that we've entered into this lifelong agreement with our spouses and with God. This is why it exclusively belongs *within* marriage.

Paul Eddy is a pastor at Woodland Hills Church in St. Paul, Minnesota. In a video Q&A with Senior Pastor Greg Boyd, he gives an excellent explanation when asked why premarital sex is wrong, and he likens having sex to signing a check:

What would be the problem in God's mind with sex prior to marriage? I think it would be this… You'd be signing a covenant that you're not in. That's just illogical.

Remember that when you sign a check, it comes from covenant-al, contractual language; my sign is my signature and that's telling someone when I hand it to them, I'm promising you: (1) this is my bank account and not someone else's; (2) there are enough funds in this check and I'm not ripping you off. They can trust my sign, my signature. Well, we are supposed to trust each other when we "sign" each other sexually with our bodies. It's a physical act that says, "I'm promising you there is a covenant to back this up."

Is it fun to write checks? Of course. You get to buy stuff. But I shouldn't write a check that I stole from my neighbor's house yester-day, or I shouldn't write a check that has my name on it when I know fully well it has no funds in that account. It's called fraud. You go to jail for that sort of stuff. It's called lying. If we realize that signing with our body with a person is no different than signing a check, we just have to ask the question, "Is it a covenant that I'm signing?" If not, I'm lying with my body. That is why I believe God always connects sex with covenant.

So it's clear that sex outside of marriage is definitely not in God's plan. Many non-believers will tell you that there's no real rea-son to wait until marriage if you don't believe in God or the cov-enantal nature of sex. If we really are just animals, then nothing's stopping us from throwing our cares to the wind and enjoying our-selves. You might be surprised to learn though that there's quite a lot of *scientific* evidence to suggest that this is a bad idea.

When you engage with someone sexually, hormones are re-leased that affect certain areas of your brain, and one of those hor-mones is oxytocin. Oxytocin is often called the "bonding hormone," and it aids in your ability to bond emotionally with your partner. It's released at the moment of orgasm to help build trust between you. This means that the emotional element of sex isn't just Christian silliness; it's built into us as organisms.

Regardless of religious or moral beliefs (unless of course you're talking about strictly patriarchal societies or arranged marriages), marriage traditionally comes about when two people spend enough time with each other to know that they're a good emotional fit. They enjoy time together over anyone else, and their personalities and interests are not only compatible, but also complement each other. So, when you find the man of your dreams and marry him, you can then use sex to deepen your emotional bond.

However, if you have sex before you get married, the oxytocin in your brain tricks you into giving a man more trust than he's actually earned. It's a counterfeit version of emotional connection because a full emotional experience with the man isn't there to back it up.

I believe this is one of the reasons divorce rates are currently at a record high, and I've personally seen the negative effects of premarital sex in many, many couples. A lot of these marriages have ended in divorce. Many of these couples are still together but getting through their issues took a tremendous amount of work. They all have one thing in common though: they used sex as a Band-Aid to cover up their problems and incompatibilities. Time and time again, you'll observe couples who seem like they can't stand each other. They fight all the time, they can't agree on anything, they often don't even enjoy spending time together...but when a particularly nasty fight turns into make-up sex, they fall in love all over again.

A woman's natural need for emotional affirmation, combined with the release of oxytocin during sex, makes premarital sex a very dangerous thing. It can lead you to trust a man who hasn't yet proven he's trustworthy. It can trick you into believing that he's a better fit for you than he actually is. It can help distract you both from serious relational problems that need to be addressed. It can lead to a marriage that was never meant to be.

One more reason to wait until you're married for sex, and to honor the covenant you'll make with your future husband, is that it means you'll have fewer sexual partners in your life (ideally just one, though premature death and divorce can of course lead to more than one marriage). If you don't hold to this core value, and several of your relationships don't end up working out, chances are good that you'll end up with a number of sexual partners. Since we bond so deeply when we have sex, moving from one partner to another involves repeatedly ripping that bond apart—breaking something that was created to last a lifetime. This can cause you to become calloused to the true meaning and importance of sex.

By no means am I saying that these callouses can't heal. I myself had multiple sexual partners before I returned to the Lord, and now I enjoy a healthy and passionate marriage. But that healing did take time, and this is another case where going outside of God's boundaries can lead to heartache and pain. It's more evidence that the Word's boundaries around sex and marriage are ones we can trust.

The Guidelines of Marriage and Sex

The unifying aspect of marriage, and the role it plays in our lives, did not change after the redemptive work of Jesus, and it certainly didn't remain cursed and strained. God doesn't want us to have miserable, broken down, disconnected relationships. He is a relational God and cares deeply about the quality and state of our unity with each other. That's why, through Jesus' sacrifice, the purpose of sex in marriage was restored back to how it was in the utopia of the Garden. And because of the redemptive work of the Holy Spirit in our lives, we no longer have to live under the curse of death, which relationally and sexually manifests as brokenness and disconnection. In this regard we are back to walking with God and living in abundance.

Just as He did in Genesis though, God still continues to place boundaries around us in order to protect us. Even though sex is a gift from God, He requires us to steward this gift with His guidance. Not all of our sexual feelings or attractions originate from or are approved by God. (I'll address some of these feelings specifically in later chapters.) A person's sex drive itself needs to be managed; thus, we need to understand the Bible's guidelines for this wonderful and powerful gift.

Feelings are ever changing and easily manipulated, depending on the season and stages of life we're in. It's very possible to feel pleasure and enjoyment while going outside of God's plan for sex; it's an error in thinking to believe otherwise. Your ability to enjoy sex outside of God's plan is not a sign that you know what's best for you. People can live in sin and like it. We can easily be deceived like Eve was if we don't trust God with our sexuality. Self-serving motives can steal from the bliss and ecstasy that sex in marriage is intended to provide for us. Pleasure is not the problem; pleasure in the context of its purpose is what should guide us.

Deciding what you believe about sexual boundaries when you're turned on and horny is setting yourself up for failure. It's akin to going to the grocery store when you just finished up at the gym and you're starving. When the sexual engines are turned on and burning hot, your hormonally designed body is in the driver's seat, and I see this issue time and again with couples that I counsel. When you're in that place, your sex drive is shouting, "SATISFY ME," because that's exactly what it was designed to do.

The most important principle to remember when trying to understand God's purpose for sex is that sex is to be expressed in love.

That's why sex is most fulfilling when it's *other-focused*. God defines the boundaries of satisfying each other's sexual desires inside of marriage. Healthy and godly sex is meant for satisfying and pleasuring your spouse. This is not, however, at the expense of our own pleasure; we just don't start with us as the center. We make loving and pleasuring them the focus. This in turn is meant to be cyclical. When our spouses are loving us in the way God intended, they are focused on our needs and solely committed to us.

If sex is modeled after Jesus and His love for the church, then it's a sacrificial dance between two people who prefer one another over anyone else. Sex is an exchange, it's about the back-and-forth flow of love—knowing what stimulates your body and mind, learning to communicate that need to your spouse, learning what stimulates *their* body and mind, and being fulfilled by that mutual exchange. Without self-control—which is the hallmark of a healthy marriage—sex then becomes perverted. It becomes about manipulation, consumption, and serving the self. Without the proper relational connections, it can become both self-focused and fear-based.

This perversion comes when Jesus' example of relationship is not the model of sexual intimacy; that's when sex becomes an idol. In other words, we shape sex using a model of a different god's design. You become what you worship. Since we know there is one true God, and any other lesser god is in fact the Father of Lies who hates us, we can clearly see that selfish sex is not of God. Self-centered sex seeks our own gratification at the expense of others. **Sex becomes abusive when dominance and fear are used to motivate instead of love.** Jesus washing the feet of His disciples is an example of Him demonstrating selfless and reciprocal love. He loved and served them, and in return they loved and served Him. He elevated the needs of others and modeled serving and sacrificial love.

God blesses sexual behavior when it follows His purpose, which is in the institution of heterosexual marriage with one spouse.

Lifelong monogamy (barring death and grounds for biblical divorce) is the boundary that Jesus placed around sex in scripture.

In Mark 10:6-8, Jesus quotes Genesis when asked about divorce and marriage. He states that marriage is between a man and woman. Sex outside of marriage (this includes any type of erotic thought life or stimulus) is immoral and considered sin. Romans 13:9, Ephesians 5:3, Galatians 5:19, and 1 Corinthians 6:13 are just a few of the scriptures you can reference regarding sex outside of marriage, and this includes both sex out of wedlock and infidelity *within* marriage. Again, sex outside of marriage is self-serving, because it emphasizes convenience over the lifelong covenant connection of marriage, and therefore, does not reflect what Jesus did for us.

In the same way God desires to be the one and only God we worship, He created sex with the intention that it exist between only one man and one woman until death separates them. Letting other people into your covenant relationship or having sex outside of a covenant relationship is like letting other gods into your life and this can result in severe damage.

Sex and the Single Woman

We all have different backgrounds and unique stories. This may be the first time you've read about sexuality in the context of your walk with Jesus. Some of you single women reading this may be completely new to the faith or may have attempted to walk a celibate life for the Lord for years, only to stumble along the way. Knowing that you're loved and adored by the Lord—even if you're currently stumbling—is key in protecting your heart and your overall emotional health. There is no condemnation or shame with Jesus, even if you've missed the mark in any of these areas in the past.

My heart is for you to understand your value and worth; He deeply loves you and desires only the best for you. If you understand what you're worth, and how much you're loved, other avenues of self-gratification and lesser pleasure will lose their grip.

If you're engaging in a sexual relationship and are unmarried, I encourage you to invite the Lord to speak to you regarding what to do in this area of your life. You are worth pursuing with honor and respect; please know that if you're having sex outside of marriage, you're selling yourself short. If you're willing to sacrifice sexual integrity before marriage, then it's all the easier to do so *after* you're married when things become more difficult.

When you engage in sexual activity outside of His protection, there is ultimately a void of satisfaction. I'll talk more about managing your sex drive later in the book but know that today is always the day of salvation. If you're in a sexual relationship outside of marriage, today the Lord has freedom for you. You don't have to go through months of behavioral management before you can go to the Lord. He has grace for you and wants to meet you where you are.

When you protect your heart and steward your boundaries through waiting, it further opens the door for being loved and respected and protected later on when you're married. In many ways you're the one who dictates how others treat you in your life, so you must ask the question: *How important is it to be treated with love and respect by the one man who will be most intimate with you?* Setting yourself up with healthy boundaries allows for much better and more fulfilling sex in the future.

Sex and the Married Woman

Married women, you are mandated by the Lord to have exotic, hot, godly sex with your husband. Why do I use the word "exotic?" Well exotic means originating in, or characteristic of, a distant foreign country. This word accurately describes sex in a kingdom-of-God-minded marriage. Philippians 3:20 says that we are citizens of heaven. We are not of this world. We are made for more than just salvation—more than simply going to heaven when we die. We reflect God and the church through loving our spouses well and walking in healthy sexual intimacy.

As we learn to love each other in a deeper capacity, God does not withhold ecstasy from our bedrooms. You are called to do more than just survive the daily grind of life; you are called to thrive in your sex life with your husband. And as vital as loyalty is, your sex life is greater than even that. When you understand the keys to keeping your mind and body committed to the Lord through loving your spouse well and cultivating deep sexual intimacy, your life will be filled with joy, satisfaction, adventure, and creativity. There is a war going on, and the enemy means to keep us (believers) away from this truth.

Prayer

I would like to offer a prayer opportunity for anyone who may feel the conviction of the Holy Spirit regarding either sex outside of marriage or sex outside of *your* marriage. God is ready and able to forgive you and empower you to walk in the healthy sexuality that He designed for you. You can pray these words if you feel led by the Holy Spirit:

Jesus, I realize that I have stepped outside the boundaries you have established for my safety. I desire to claim all the authority in my life for which you died and were resurrected. Please forgive me for having sex outside of marriage. I receive your forgiveness, cleansing, healing, and restoration. Please forgive me for mistrusting you and allowing the enemy to distort my role as your daughter. I receive your forgiveness today. I invite the power of the Holy Spirit to cleanse me and set me in the right direction. Thank you for being a loving father who was waiting for me to turn to you. You are the same yesterday, today, and forever. You are a kind and loving God, and through our relationship you will empower me to walk in truth. Amen!

Chapter Three

Your Sexy Body

"Knowledge is love and light and vision."

—Helen Keller

You have a Sex Drive

Surprise! Let's all just take a moment and thank Jesus. Just lift your hands and wave your white handkerchief in the air like you just don't care. Hallelujah. Glory. Your body was made for hot lovin' and it was *all* God's idea! Even if you're single and you liken having a sex drive to being a tormented cat in heat, thank God you were made for deep physical connection. If you've struggled with your sex drive or with intimacy, then let's lift off that shame blanket.

Repeat after me: *"God made my sex drive and called it good! Having a sex drive is not a sign that something is wrong with me!"*

There are many books out there on female anatomy and biology, but when mentoring women of all ages I find too often that they lack even a basic understanding of their own body. I believe this is due to the rigidness and fear associated with sexual education. So, here's some basic information that you might find helpful in understanding your sex drive.

Your Menstrual Cycle

Most women begin puberty around age nine to twelve (though plenty of women fall before or after these averages) and go through a series of changes over about four years. And let me say, I'm so thankful those awkward years are behind me—those precarious years of falling over things and not knowing where my backside started or ended. (Although now that I think about it, not much has changed for me in that regard!)

Girls can expect a lack of coordination, breast growth, the first appearance of pubic hair, body odor emerging from crevices they didn't know they had, and that oh-so-glorious little friend called the menstrual cycle makes her first appearance of many. Our genetics, nutrition, ethnicity, and even weight play a role in how and when we reach our milestones in sexual development. I was overweight from a young age, which caused these years to be especially painful. My father was overweight as well. At the time of my first period, I feared that I had inherited my father's breasts.

All right, back to the basics. After a woman reaches puberty, she begins to ovulate. Ovulation is the process in which an egg (sometimes more than one in the case of twins) is released from one ovary, which is a reproductive organ found in the pelvic region. Women have two ovaries, and on occasion both ovaries can release an egg at the same time, but it's rare. When ovulating, some women experience spotting or minor discomfort in their lower abdomen while others have no symptoms at all. If that egg is fertilized by a sperm as it travels down the fallopian tube, the fertilized egg attaches to the lining of the uterus and pregnancy occurs. An organ called the placenta then develops, and this transfers nutrients and oxygen from the mother to the fetus.

Menstruation is when the shedding of the endometrium (the lining of the uterus) occurs. The purpose of the endometrium is to nourish a baby during pregnancy. Increased levels of estrogen and progesterone help thicken its walls in order to prepare for this, but if the egg is not fertilized and no pregnancy occurs, it sheds. This uterine wall, along with blood and mucus from the uterus and cervix, flow out of the vagina. This is what causes menstruation.

Since the endometrium doesn't shed during pregnancy, pregnant women don't experience menstruation. (Spotting and bleeding are both possible during this time, but any vaginal bleeding during pregnancy is the product of something other than a menstrual cycle and should be discussed with a doctor.)

The average menstrual cycle lasts twenty-eight days. The cycle starts with the first day of one period and ends with the first day of the next period. On average, a woman will ovulate on day fourteen, but again, all these times can vary. A woman is likely to become pregnant if she has sex during ovulation or even a few days before, since sperm can survive in the uterus for up to five days. For those of you who have sex on your period as a means of birth control, take note that this might not be very effective. If you combine an extra long-lasting sperm with an extra-short ovulation period, pregnancy becomes possible.

Possible Sexual Arousal During Your Cycle

Some women are unaware of the role that hormones play in our sex drives. Estrogen and progesterone levels surge and lessen throughout our cycle, and will sometimes send our bodies the signal that it's time to turn on some R&B and light some candles. Researchers have found that peak sexual arousal can occur close to ovulation, with a second peak occurring two days before menstruation when progesterone is low, and a third peak around day four of the period. Not every woman falls into this exact pattern, which is why it's helpful to learn about your own body and become aware of your hormonal patterns so that you can better understand your need to listen to Barry White at certain times of the month. (Personally, I always liken the two days before my period to a bartender yelling out, "LAST CALL!" before closing time.)

Keeping Record of Your Body Changes

I highly recommend that you chart your menstrual cycles. You can download an app on your phone or keep a journal of the first day of your period and when you feel any symptoms of ovulation, of which there are many (like light cramping, egg-white-like discharge from your vagina, and increased desire to have sex). Again, this will occur about fourteen days into your cycle. One way you can track your cycle a little more precisely is to measure your temperature first thing in the morning, which is called charting your basal body temperature.

In fact, there are a number of methods many women use when they're trying to get pregnant, and they all apply here. However, as a good practice in the beginning, try to simply keep track of the days you menstruate. Twenty-eight days is the average cycle length, but since cycles are different and range from twenty-one to thirty-four days, it's important to consistently track.

Your overall health plays a big part in your fertility. If you begin to track your periods, you can speak with a doctor or health-care professional about them when you go for annual pap smear exams. (A pap smear is an exam that includes gathering a sample of discharge from your vagina to test for cervical cancer). Knowing your body is important for your overall health and being aware of what your body is doing will help you communicate any changes to a doctor.

Even after you have an idea of what your menstrual cycle looks like, I encourage you to create a habit of tracking. This is beneficial for both single and married women. If you're single you'll learn how your body is talking to you through hormonal changes, and if you're married you'll know when you're most fertile for conception. Irregularities in your menstruation can sometimes point to health issues that need to be discussed with a doctor, so in either case it's good to track everything.

As you learn to steward your sex drive, understanding that you're naturally more aroused around certain times of the month will help to demystify what you feel. If you're single, this information can help you redirect your attention, and if you're married, you can fully utilize these peak days. Basically, the more attuned you are with the hormonal aspect of your sex drive, the more you can keep it within God's boundaries and take advantage of it. Knowing about these natural phases also helps to dispel the lie that the urge to dim the lights and light some incense is a bad thing.

What is an Orgasm?

Now that we've covered the basics of your menstrual cycle, let's talk about orgasms. Procreation is one thing, but another important aspect of sex is *pleasure*. The most physically pleasurable part of sex is the orgasm. Let me repeat that fact: **Pleasure most definitely involves reaching orgasm during sex.** The orgasm isn't the *only* aspect of sex that's pleasurable, and it's possible to have a satisfying sexual experience without one. In fact, there are many reasons why it can be more difficult for some women to reach orgasm, and you should never feel pressured to be some sort of orgasmic machine. But, if you ask me, orgasms are where it's at. They're the icing on the cake. And I like icing.

The interesting thing about them, though, is that they don't really play a part in procreation. Some studies show that having an orgasm can potentially help aid in getting pregnant, but by no means are they strictly necessary. I truly believe the Lord designed orgasms as a reflection of the ecstasy of unity, meant to further strengthen our connection with our spouses. The orgasm is a great reminder that we are not just functional creatures, but relational ones who long for depth and enjoyment. We want to be fruitful and multiply, but sometimes we just want to have a party for a party's sake.

So, what exactly is an orgasm? A woman experiences an orgasm when there is proper stimulus of the erogenous zones of the body, with the focus being on the clitoris. Along with physical stimulation, mental arousal aids in reaching orgasm. You've probably heard that the brain is the largest sexual organ, and it's true; the majority of sexual stimulus comes from the mind. Some therapists who specialize in sexual health believe it plays into approximately *eighty* percent of a woman's arousal. In other words, to achieve an orgasm, both your body and your mind must be stimulated. The clitoris certainly helps, but that big sexy brain of yours does most of the heavy lifting.

God designed us with erogenous zones to stimulate sexual arousal when touched, and He designed us with an imagination to house erotic thoughts toward our spouses. And through physical stimulation and an erotic mental state, we reach that orgasm. Some women who are married have never experienced an orgasm, and there are various reasons for this. These women may have grown up in an environment where sex was shameful; they may have been abused; they may lack the hormones that aid in sexual arousal; or perhaps they don't know how to communicate their needs during sex because they've never explored what feels good to them.

When approaching orgasm, your body goes through a series of automatic responses, where it talks to itself and starts firing up all the right cylinders needed for the orgasm. For example, your hormones talk to your vaginal walls and they begin to change. Blood flow increases, the hormone estrogen causes fluid to be released from the Bartholin gland, and as a result the vaginal walls lubricate themselves. Lubrication is needed for the penis to easily penetrate the vagina and cause pressure without pain. Penetration during sex does not necessarily guarantee an orgasm, but it can aid in it.

Along with mental arousal, stimulation of the clitoris—which sits above your vagina, at the anterior end of the vulva— is what produces an orgasm. When stimulation reaches its climax, your pubococcygeus or "PC" muscle goes through a series of contractions. The resulting feeling can be a whole-body high, the pinnacle of physical ecstasy. I'll remind you once more that this was all God's idea and His gift to us. How we value this gift will dictate if it produces health in our lives.

On top of orgasms not being required for procreation, it's also interesting to note that God gave us the ability to have an orgasm without the physical involvement of another person. He could have easily designed our bodies in such a way that achieving orgasm *required* fitting together with another body. An orgasmic kind of Lego set, if you will. Believe it or not, having access to your lady parts 24/7 is also part of His perfect design.

Masturbation

Masturbation is the act of erotically stimulating your own genitals with the intent of causing an orgasm. Masturbation is not a sin in itself, and the shame surrounding it causes nothing but fear and confusion. It's under the umbrella of sexuality, and just like sex it can aid in a fruitful stewardship within the boundaries of God's design, or it can lead to destructive, sinful activity outside of His design. However, we'll talk more about this in a bit.

Let me state it plainly, just to be really clear: **Masturbation has a place in our sexual relationships.** It's extremely helpful when you're expressing yourself to your spouse or guiding them in sexual discovery. It's meant to be shared and used as a tool to deepen your intimacy with each other, as an aid within the context of marriage. As a married woman, this is part of your ongoing adventure with your spouse. Even this was by the design of our God so that we could better learn how to pleasure our spouses and how they may pleasure us.

Now, I know there are single women reading this book, and maybe even women who have experienced the loss of a spouse, and they now face this question: If masturbation is a gift from God himself, is it okay to masturbate? I'll address all you single ladies in various ways as this book progresses, so keep reading.

Regarding widowed women, I just want to take a moment to speak to your process. In a perfect world, you would only experience the loss of a spouse at a ripe old age when you're well past your sexual peak. If you're an eighty-year-old widow, masturbation may no longer be an issue. I surely pray that my body is a supernatural love machine well into my golden years, but from what I hear it tends to taper down as the clock turns.

Some of you may be widowed and unsure if you will remarry, however, and yet you still have a sexual appetite because of those years of godly sex with your husband. The Holy Spirit is fully able to meet you in this place and guide you through this time in your life. I don't believe there is any condemnation if you masturbate while thinking of your husband. I'm not just wholeheartedly condoning masturbation, though; it's up to you to pray into this aspect of your life and ask yourself if it's keeping you from moving past your grief.

God may desire to bring you into another relationship and masturbating could inhibit this. It could also inhibit His desire to bring comfort through the Holy Spirit because you are leaning on physical comfort. As it is in every situation, if your heart and mind aren't in the right place, masturbation can feed into a cycle of isolation and depression, and this can be especially true when masturbation reminds you that your spouse is no longer present to share in sexual intimacy. Basically, everyone's story is unique, and it's up to you to bring this before God in prayer and look closely at what fruit it will bring in your life.

A similar situation that's worth mentioning is one where a husband is incapacitated and unable to have sex. He may be injured or have a terminal illness or disease that renders him incapable of engaging you physically. Once again, it's something you'll need to pray about. Masturbation in this case could act as a perfect way for you and your husband to remain intimate in your own way, or it could work to drive you further apart.

I will say that it is a huge sacrifice to become a caregiver to a sexually incapable spouse when you're still primed for intercourse. This sacrifice is beautiful, and I truly believe that godly caregivers in these circumstances are some of the unsung heroes of the faith. A woman in this situation gives herself to the covenant of marriage and sacrifices a part of herself that others take for granted, all while carrying the heart of the Lord through her longsuffering.

Church culture does a poor job of celebrating people in these circumstances. We tend to focus on praising the gifted and neglect to honor men and women who pour their lives out for each other in sacrificial ways. If you're in this situation, it can't be easy, but always know that your sacrifice has not gone unnoticed.

My Story

In my house growing up, masturbation was a dirty and shameful thing. My mother never spoke to me about sex. When I was young and beginning to discover my own body, she would scold me for my questions and my curiosity. I certainly don't blame her or hold anything against her, as I've come to realize that her fear of sex stemmed from being sexually abused by multiple men when she was younger. At the time, however, her reactions caused me to hide anything and everything related to sex. I was alone in my discovery.

My father knew that it was a painful subject for her and tried to fill in a few of the gaps by giving me the ABC's of sex, but his teaching was very lacking. I was informed of the more technical side of sexuality, and don't get me wrong—this was certainly helpful. Children need to hear both the voices of their mother and father when learning about their bodies and the amazing gift of sex. There are, however, more intimate conversations that a girl needs to have with her mother or a mother figure. There were many questions that I knew he couldn't answer and many that I didn't feel comfortable asking a man, even my own father. Being able to talk to someone of the same gender about sex is important, especially at such a vulnerable pubescent age.

It's important to state here that my curiosity was not a sin. Proverbs 25:2 (NIV) says, *"It is the glory of God to conceal a matter; to search out a matter is the glory of kings."* I love how the Message Bible paraphrases this verse, *"God delights in concealing things; scientists delight in discovering things."* We are designed to explore and search out the wonders of God's creations. Our bodies and how they work are part of this wonderful creation. I was made to discover Eden. Without proper guidance, however, my exploration opened the door for much pain and bondage.

Scolding a child for masturbating can damage them greatly. It's a reaction of fear and sows only shame. There are appropriate ways to guide a child back into God's boundaries while they're developing and discovering their sex drive. I believe the best way is to educate children on how their bodies are designed and what milestones lay ahead of them.

We can explain how masturbation is a natural part of a growing sex drive, but there are healthier ways to manage this growth. Sex is meant for mutual enjoyment, not isolation. Sexual tension was not designed to torment us, but to ultimately bring health and excitement to marriage. This sets the foundation for many years of sexual learning.

None of this was common knowledge within my childhood home, but the outside world was very different. Outside my childhood home, the environment I grew up in was steeped in feminism. My parents pastored a small church in a rural community in the mountains of Northern California, and let's just say we stood out a little.

Although my parents were fearful about sex and consequently missed an opportunity to educate me, I was surrounded by feminist friends and teachers who were more than happy to provide a welcoming environment to discuss sex. Their worldview was drastically different from my own Christian upbringing, but I was looking for education and understanding and they provided it.

To the great credit of these feminists, their desire to educate and welcome discussion was actually very godly. I don't want to overgeneralize or alienate any readers who consider themselves feminists. There are many feminist Christians, and this is certainly not a dig at their beliefs regarding the liberation of women. This group of feminists, however, had a non-Christ-centered worldview that was counter to God's plans for me.

In this environment I learned about how my body was made and that my emotional needs were legitimate, which were healthy lessons. The error was in how and where I was told to meet those needs. I was taught that I was the best guide in meeting my sexual needs. There is a grain of truth in this, because in the context of marriage you can communicate what feels best to you. But feminism took this idea to the max, and I was told that sexual pleasure was mine to seek out in any way I saw fit. The message was: masturbate whenever you want, sleep with whoever makes you feel safe, and embrace free love as long as you use protection and don't get in any weird vans with middle-aged guys with mustaches. It's your body, and you have every right to seek happiness. Again, it's a partial truth.

With this new feminist mindset, I developed a poor and unhealthy management of my sex drive. I began masturbating often and it wasn't long before the idea of seeking out a sexual encounter was strong in my mind, which only managed to confuse and frustrate me even more. I reached a peak of both my sexual exploration and my separation from anything having to do with Christ and the church, and I was absolutely miserable. Feminism taught me to know my body, but it failed to tell me why I had a body. This was not the liberation I'd been longing for in my quest for empowerment.

What's so Bad About Masturbation?

If our bodies were designed for sexual expression, then why is masturbation outside of marriage unhealthy? This is a question many women have asked me, and it's a great question. I myself didn't learn the answer until I was in my mid-twenties, when I met a couple who led a sexual wholeness ministry. What they taught me has been confirmed time and time again throughout my life.

Like I explained in the previous chapter about sex, we are meant to find fulfillment by pleasuring our spouse. We are created for wholehearted devotion to one God, and in the same way we are meant for wholehearted intimacy with one spouse. Sexual fulfillment comes when we are creatively exploring sex in marriage. It's cyclical. I pour my affection and care into you, and you seek to fulfill my sexual needs. You learn my body and I learn yours in a safe and Spirit-filled environment.

We have this natural sex drive so that when we go through the mundane and even difficult times in our marriages, we have something to help bring us back together, something that physically and spiritually bonds us again. God intends us to protect and cultivate our sex life within the safe boundaries of sex. And remember, the idea of two becoming one through sex isn't just Christian fluff, either; biologically there are hormones released during sex that not only cause pleasure but also cause emotional bonding. As much as our culture wants to tell us that sexual monogamy is an old, outdated, man-invented idea meant to oppress women, this is the furthest from the biblical truth.

In the animal kingdom, everything is driven by uncontrolled sexual instinct. God did not create animals with the ability to make logical choices. When their hormones drive them to mate, they find a mate who will produce the strongest offspring. But God didn't design us that way. God created us with a sex drive that's entirely under our control. We have the ability to exercise constraint, or to choose a partner based on much more than physical prowess. We were made to do more than just procreate.

You are not an animal. You are a daughter of the Creator of the Universe. The idea that we're all purely animalistic, void of sexual self-control, and that masturbation is a call we must heed, is false. When you believe that your impulses are simply part of your physiology, and that it's wise and even necessary to satisfy them at all costs, you will find yourself unfulfilled. This is embracing an ideology that is not biblical and does not reflect God's design.

Singleness and Masturbation

Masturbating when you're single may release hormones and cause a chemical high, but through it you create a cyclical pattern where you pour only into yourself. Since about eighty percent of arousal and successful orgasm comes from erotic stimulation of your mind, this leaves you susceptible to unhealthy fantasies. Masturbating alone creates false senses of comfort, excitement, and gratification. Filling your life with fantasy keeps you away from the reality Jesus wants you to live in. I'll cover the subject of fantasy in greater detail in the next chapter.

This self-fulfilling pattern, and the isolation that comes from it, bleeds out into every aspect of your life: how you interact with your peers, how you engage in entertainment, how you view yourself, and ultimately it affects your relationship with the Holy Spirit. If you're stuck in this pattern, the Lord absolutely still loves you and is always actively pursuing you, but He's hindered from fully working in your life. Without surrendering your sex drive to Him, He can't strengthen you through it.

Many believe a great lie that it's impossible to manage our sex drives without masturbation. Some believe it's the only possible way to curb our primal desires and stop ourselves from jumping on the first hunky guy we come across. The truth is that God designed nothing in this physical world that we can't steward with His help, and that includes our physical bodies.

Whether you're an adolescent or an adult, you may wake up aroused after an erotic dream, or you may become so hormonally charged around the time of ovulation that even wearing tight clothes is stimulating. As it is with men as well, sometimes your hormones will cry out like a fat dog locked outside on steak night. As we've established, this is your body doing its job and doing it well. What matters is what habits stem from these desires. Masturbating a few times while trying to figure out how your sex drive works is one thing, especially if you're a pubescent teen. It's another to habitually self-satisfy without the guidance of the Holy Spirit. I'll talk more about managing your sex drive through godly principles in Chapter Seven.

Marriage and Masturbation

If you developed a habitual pattern of masturbating when you were single, I'm willing to bet this pattern didn't dissipate when you got married. In fact, I'm also willing to bet it's introduced intimacy issues that have put a strain on your sexual relationship with your spouse. Relying so much on self-satisfying without your husband's involvement has likely left an intimacy deficit in your marriage.

Part of the problem is that many women are under the impression that masturbation outside of marriage is bad merely because it's "against the rules," and that your marriage certificate comes with a free pass to please yourself whenever you want, guilt-free. They mistakenly believe that marriage is like a golden ticket of sexual gratification handed to you by Lily Wonka herself.

If this is an issue for you, continuing to masturbate will only perpetuate the habit. If you choose to stop now, it will be the first step toward addressing the issue and it will motivate you to open up with your husband. In the same way that waiting on sex until marriage is likely to make a couple decide *pretty quick* whether or not they should get hitched, denying yourself of instant self-gratification through masturbation will make it much easier to bring your needs to him and get to the root of the intimacy issues between you.

(I mean there's nothing like a screaming sex drive to make you cry out to the Lord, "Do what you want with me, this problem needs to be *solved!*")

Choosing to live in passivity and hopelessness, however, can result in something even worse than damaged intimacy with your husband. When you justify your habits and never make a change, you cast yourself deeper and deeper into isolation, which is the foot in the door that the enemy needs to wrench his way through to influence your life.

A common justification is that solo masturbation is okay as long as you're thinking of your husband. And hey, I won't deny that if you're going to think of someone while you masturbate, it should definitely be your husband. Nevertheless, you can never shrug away the fact that this is still not the same as communicating with your husband about your sexual needs as God intended.

I'm also willing to bet that the image of your husband in your mind will inevitably start to change over time—a little less chunk here, some chiseled abs there, maybe replace that wispy little growth with a full lumberjack beard, throw in a British accent for good measure—until the image that turns you on is a full-on fabrication in no way grounded in reality. If you're disconnected intimately, the world in your head becomes a counterfeit.

You just need to understand that the comfort and relief you feel when you masturbate will always be false and temporary. An orgasm is more fulfilling when it's shared. That's why God created it. If you don't allow the Holy Spirit, who is The Comforter, restore this area of your marriage, unsatisfying sex will only be the beginning of your problems with your husband. See this pattern as a big red flag and turn the other way.

I know it takes great humility to seek out help in this area. It's not an easy conversation to have, but if you do get help, God will meet you there and bless you for it. Stepping up and addressing these issues takes courage and God will never fail to honor you for that courage.

You are not a failure if you've slipped into these patterns. The lure of masturbation is something we all have to face, and this issue is a common one. Bring it before God and initiate brave communication with your spouse, and you'll be back on track to building sexual intimacy in your marriage.

Guidelines to Consider for Masturbation

The issue of solo masturbation in marriage is one of communication. Therefore, on the subject of *any* healthy masturbation within marriage, communication with your spouse is the most important thing. Some couples share in a mutual agreement that no masturbation will occur under any circumstances outside the bedroom. Others may allow plenty of circumstances and both share in the pleasure of it, as long as they maintain a mutual trust and exercise self-control. There's actually more freedom in this regard than you might imagine; two empowered people who trust each other fully are open to much discovery.

For women especially, it's important to understand what feels good and how to communicate that to your spouse. Sometimes both parties can feel a lot of pressure to perform when they're both trying to navigate this whole lovemaking thing. (New couples, you likely know this better than anyone.)

One way to aid in this process is to privately explore. It's not a sin to stimulate yourself with the desire to discover what you enjoy so that you can communicate it to your husband. As we've been learning, mindset, purpose, and inclusion of the Holy Spirit are everything here. I encounter women who are completely disconnected from their bodies because of the fear that religion has placed on them. They're ruled by restrictions, they have no idea how their husbands might pleasure their bodies because they think all sexual expression and discovery is sinful. These women have missed the purpose of sexual expression entirely: to build intimacy with your spouse.

Having a prayerful time of self-discovery while thinking about your husband, then sharing what you've discovered so you can experience better lovemaking, is in no way sinful. Fear is not our guide when it comes to sex. The God who created your vagina, though? That's the guy in charge. And He very much wants you to understand how it operates, so that your relationship with your husband can be both fruitful and blissful. I'll add here that some people reading this might be uncomfortable with the idea of this kind of self-discovery. If this is the case, invite your husband into an easygoing, no-pressure lovemaking session where he helps you explore. Communication is always the key.

Extraneous Circumstances

There are other situations in which masturbation can be beneficial within a marriage, even when it's done in private. You may be going through a season where you're away for a lengthy amount of time because of work, an emergency in the family, or any number of situations where you're both separated for an extended period. In a case like this, both husband and wife may think of each other and masturbate while they're apart, frequently communicating with each other about how it arouses them. This can bring a couple closer together when they're reunited, be a tool in building and maintaining intimacy, and even act as a safeguard.

The enemy could easily use an extended time apart to cause one of you to stumble back into unhealthy practices such as pornography usage or indulging in isolating fantasies. That's why this sort of sexual play can be so beneficial in strengthening you both during longer times of separation. When two people trust each other and engage in a way that blesses each other, the Lord blesses them both. When physical proximity is a barrier, creativity is allowed. Like with everything, having a plan of action and talking about what it will look like when you're apart is crucial. Realize that you both have sex drives that can sometimes lead to moments of weaknesses, and you can protect your connection by creating a plan to stay intimate even when you are apart.

Injury and illness are also examples of extraneous circumstances where you're temporarily unable to engage sexually with your spouse. Perhaps your husband has pulled a groin muscle and can't have sex for fear of further damaging himself. He may find great joy in watching you pleasure yourself, and through your pleasure you can both share in the ecstasy.

I think you're starting to see the point I'm trying to make about how masturbation can be part of God's plan for a healthy marriage. The key is to have shared sexual experiences that lead to deeper intimacy where two people are engaging in empowered and joyful expression.

Guidelines for Sexual Intimacy

Now, let's transition out of masturbation talk and back into sex with a spouse. There may be boundaries around sex within a marriage, but between two creative, spontaneous, Spirit-filled believers, there's plenty of room for exciting sex. Heaven knows that technology and the Internet offer a plethora of options and advice for enhancing your lovemaking, but I'm often asked what is and isn't appropriate in the bedroom. How adventurous is too adventurous?

The following is my advice, but it's by no means exhaustive or exclusive, nor should it take the place of prayer and communication with your spouse.

As always, the goal here is to learn what you each enjoy and grow in intimacy. Adventurous lovemaking only works when it's safe, entirely mutual, and never manipulative. I've seen married couples try to spice up their time in the bedroom without first dealing with root communication and intimacy problems and this only caused more disconnect.

The most fruitful and fulfilling sex life comes from first allowing the Lord to address any issues that are acting as barriers in your marriage. Desiring to turn up the heat in bed needs to come as the fruit of wanting to strengthen your connection with your spouse—not of wanting to fix a connection that's weak or broken.

Using sex this way is a misguided way of fixing your problems, and the act of searching out new ways to make love without first having that connection can quickly become an idol. An idol is anything we turn into a source of empowerment other than God. Recklessly chasing your next sexual thrill can become your new god, or your new spouse. Play in marriage is key to a healthy sex life, but only when you and your husband are already deeply intimate, and it should never come at the cost of one of you feeling unsafe and unloved.

You can rest in where you are and what the Lord is doing through your own marriage without falling into the trap of comparing yourself to others. Some people *love* to brag about their sex lives and how adventurous they are. These people like to be seen in a certain light, especially since an active sex life is often associated with youth and vitality in our culture. Those who brag about their sex life, however, often fail to include the cost of a healthy sexual relationship. Building sexual intimacy is like climbing a mountain;

it's exciting, but it takes a lot of discipline and courage. The rewards are great, but conquering that mountain comes at the cost of hard work.

Anything worth fighting for in the kingdom of God is beautiful and costly. If a married woman brags to you about her sex life and doesn't mention the work and sacrifice she and her husband have invested in their relationship, chances are she's covering up for her insecurities.

That's not to say you can never mention your sex life; sharing cute stories and creative tips with your friends is fine, provided your friends are comfortable with it. Spilling out inappropriate details and acting like you and your husband are God's gift to sex is the problem. So, when you hear this sort of thing, don't buy the bull. Be secure in your own sex life. Understand that no one has ever had a perfect, movie-star-style sex life. Sometimes sex is like a gourmet meal, and other times it's more like a quick trip to the Costco food court. This is the adventure of sex. Sure, we aim for gourmet, but sometimes it's hotdogs for dinner, and there's nothing wrong with hotdogs.

Understanding Your Filter: A Liz Parable

When I was in my early twenties, I would often seek the advice of a spiritual father of mine named Charlie. Charlie was, and still is, the administrator of a very large church. The man is to numbers as Michelangelo is to ceilings. Charlie and his wife Julie helped me tremendously during this period of my life by opening their home to me and offering me unending wisdom. I frequently found myself sitting at their dinner table, asking for advice about various life decisions.

One night we were talking about finances and Charlie offered some advice. He told me that I should consider getting one or two credit cards. I could use them for my common monthly expenses like groceries and gas, as long as I paid them off monthly so that I didn't rack up any interest charges or debt. This would start to build my credit, which would help me make larger purchases down the line.

I nodded and told him it was a good idea and that I would definitely look into it...but what he didn't know was that inside I was doing the mambo and already daydreaming of my first shopping spree at Target. Like, you know those contests that used to be on TV, where they let a person run around a department store for sixty seconds, shoving everything they could into shopping carts before the buzzer sounded?

Well, my first trip to Target wasn't quite that bad, but it was pretty close. Charlie, in his great fatherly trust, didn't know (because I didn't tell him) that I'd grown up in a home where credit cards were our lifesavers, sometimes the only reason we had all the basic necessities. I mean, we were a dirt-poor ministry family in a Podunk town. Subconsciously, I believed that a credit card was *made* to be perpetually maxed out. Instead of being used to build credit and make large purchases possible, I thought they were to be depended on to help keep us afloat. Though of course, because of all the interest we paid, they ultimately made us poorer than ever.

Charlie's advice was wise and meant to help prepare me for the future. He wanted me to practice self-control and to build trust with creditors, which later would have huge benefits. But my filter was off. Instead of seeing credit cards for what they were, I saw them as license to go beyond my budget and far beyond his advice. Because of my experiences with them earlier in life, I completely missed this valuable lesson and instead racked up a lot of debt.

I also missed an opportunity to learn how to solve this problem. If I had gone to Charlie right when I realized I was in trouble, he would have walked me through it, and I would have come away with perhaps an even more valuable lesson than the one he first tried to teach me. However, I felt shame, and because of it, I kept my debt a secret from Charlie. So instead of turning things around right then and there, things only got worse, and it was a long time before I was able to pay off that debt.

This is a great example of how our past experiences can color our perception and affect our future, especially when it comes to certain liberties. I was given freedom with those credit cards and I abused it. This is important to understand in the next section as I talk about creativity and play in the bedroom.

If you don't live in a healthy marriage of trust and connection, it's all too easy to take sexual freedom and use it for your own self-ish ambitions. The advice I give in these next pages is meant only to enhance your connection; I'm certainly not giving you license to go beyond wisdom or the direction of the Lord. These are tools and depending entirely on any of them is not the goal. You can use a hammer to build a house, but you can't live in a hammer.

Turn up the Heat

Sex does not have to be a dreary, dutiful thing; play and creativity in the bedroom form the bedrock of a healthy marriage. Learning how to joyfully come together and have fun with your husband will keep you bonded and aligned with God's will for your marriage. It's the glue that keeps you tightly knit together as you muscle through life's ups and downs. There are few things that would delight the enemy more than robbing you of your joy in sex. Joyful sex means sacrificial pleasure that creates unity, and naturally he doesn't like that very much. He wanted to destroy it in the garden of Eden and he's after your paradise in the Lord as well, the place God created for you to dwell in His goodness.

If you allow your joy to be stolen, hopelessness and isolation won't be far behind. Creativity is the very best weapon in your fight for sexual joy and connection. Creativity refocuses you on new ways to love your husband instead of on the circumstances that may be warring against you. Yes, that's right: **Play in lovemaking is an act of spiritual warfare.**

One element of play that's important is humor. It helps to diffuse any tension and creates a relaxed and comfortable atmosphere. One night my husband and I were getting ready for bed and a few seconds after I turned off the lights, he started giggling. When I turned them back on, he was lying next to me, turned away. When he rolled over to face me, he was sporting a pair of swimmer's goggles. He said, "sex goggles!" and then burst into laughter. It's become a running joke in our sex life.

In the next few sections I'm going to cover some of the ways a married couple can spice things up in the bedroom. Single ladies, I hope you're still reading, and I hope you stick with me here even if this isn't relevant in your immediate life. Remember that my goal with this book is to instill knowledge and understanding wherever you may be.

Married ladies, I can't stress enough that whatever you bring into your marriage needs to exclusively be for both you and your husband. It needs to arouse both of you and only point you toward one another. If you feel any pressure from your husband, don't partake, and make sure not to pressure him, either. Always remember that this is about joy and discovery, about building intimacy. If either party feels at any time that their comfort and safety are being compromised, they should never hesitate to boldly say, "No thank you."

It's also important to understand that we all have different personalities and that you should feel secure in your marriage bed whether you use all of these tips or none of them. Never feel pressure to change if you're both happy where you are; God will love and care for your marriage even if you and your husband aren't currently interested in exploring new things.

One last thing before we start, there are two outstanding books I'd like to recommend for those who want to educate themselves further on sex in general, but especially for those who want to spice up their marriage: A Celebration of Sex by Dr. Douglas E. Rosenau and Sheet Music by Dr. Kevin Leman. The first clue that you can trust the knowledge they offer? Both doctors look very happy in their pictures on the back covers of their books. These two books brought life and creativity to my marriage, especially during years when my husband and I were overcoming a lot of issues in our sex lives. They helped us focus on the solutions God had for us, rather than living in shame and fear and focusing on what was wrong. They're jam-packed with wisdom regarding God's love and design, and I can't possibly recommend them highly enough.

Sex With Aid

Lingerie and other skimpy clothing is a fun and exciting way for you to feel confident in enticing your husband. It's perfect for bringing on trips or utilizing when you're feeling a bit frumpy. Throw a bikini on and jump into bed before your husband does, then sit back and watch the sparks fly. And even better, you can be thrifty! An expensive, flowy nighty from Victoria's Secret is all well and good, but nothing is better than landing a good deal on the kind of sexy two-piece bathing suit that I would never in a million years wear in public.

As we touched on earlier, some women find it hard to reach orgasm for various reasons. A sex aid, such as a vibrator, can be extremely helpful in achieving orgasm with your spouse. This idea seems very taboo for many women, but I encourage you to consider it with an open mind. Media portrayal of vibrators may paint a specific and rather intimidating picture of what this type of sex toy looks like, but in reality, many are quite low-profile and come in a variety of shapes that aren't phallic. Amazon is a great and discrete source of items such as vibrators, lubricants, and so on. You can buy whatever you want in the privacy of your own home without needing to browse your local sex shop, which may be a little overwhelming for some women.

Perhaps most importantly, if you and your husband agree to using a sex aid, I encourage you to be the one who seeks it out and buys it. Like masturbation, this will be a tool to use with your husband in order to deepen intimacy and enhance your connection. Also like masturbation, you will be the one who communicates what is pleasurable and how your body is responding. This is why it's important to choose something that you think will work best. It's also empowering to make an educated decision about what you want in the bedroom and to bring that to your spouse. Just remember to keep an open dialogue with your spouse and with the Holy Spirit, and pray for discernment regarding its purpose and frequency of use.

Even if you have no problems reaching orgasm, just the act of buying something like this can work to spice things up. More than once someone has told me that they bought a vibrator but ultimately ended up leaving it in a drawer and rarely using it. However, the simple act of bringing it into the bedroom— discussing it with their spouse and being open to using it—got things moving again. The mere attempt to bring excitement into their sex lives was exciting in and of itself.

Lubricants and massage oils are available Online or even at the grocery store, and these are more important than many women realize. They open up many avenues of pleasure, whether through more comfortable sex, sensual massage, or (ideally) a mix of both. If you're feeling adventurous, massage oils with silly names are particularly fun to buy from a sex shop or Online store, but simple, organic oils like coconut oil work as well. If you buy unscented oil, it can be fun to add a few drops of essential oils for some fragrance.

Always do some research before you try new things. If you're trying to conceive, for example, it's helpful to know that most lubricants slow down sperm and lower your chances of getting pregnant, so you'll want to find a brand that's fertility-friendly. Coconut oil is perfect for massages but when mixed with a condom it can increase the chance of breakage. Some essential oils may cause a burning sensation when applied to the skin (no peppermint oil on the nether regions, please). Remember that when it comes to what is and isn't safe in this regard, be sure to look it up.

One note about purchasing sexual aids. I've been told by married friends that some Online shops are preferable to brick and mortar stores if you've had an issue with pornography or feel uncomfortable examining these kinds of things in front of other people. There seems to be a spectrum between raunchy shops connected to sexual depravity and classier stores. Some websites use hand drawn illustrations rather than images of people having sex, which is more educational and less stimulating than the pornographic images seen in some promotional materials. It's important to find a place where you feel safe and comfortable buying these sorts of aids.

Sex in Other Locations

Some couples think nothing is better than the rush of having sex in an odd place—the woods, their cars, or any number of secluded places. This is a great example of how something that turns one woman on might not be so appealing to another. To me, this sounds about as fun as showing up at school in your underwear.

I do, however, have some adrenaline junky friends and they love the adventure and the risk. With risk comes reward...but naturally, risk can also come with unwanted results. One of my friends got hot and bothered in the woods one day, and she and her husband decided to quite literally get down and dirty. All was well until a few hours later when they began to have severe poison oak reactions in...places.

As horrible as that sounds, I do admire that they were meeting each other's needs by finding an interesting, private location to express their passion. If you like the idea of sex in strange places, just make sure that you are truly alone. Some people get off on the risk of being caught, but I can't advocate sex in any place where another person might find you, especially considering the legal aspect. A jail cell does not sound like a fun and sexy place.

Sex and Technology

Another great tool is the use of technology: video chatting, messaging, recorded videos, photos, and so on. Texting your spouse a hot love note while he's at work is a great way to get his attention and stoke the flames a little. Even though you're apart, it's essentially engaging in foreplay; being descriptive about what you'd like to do later when he's home gets you both in the creative flow. Videos and live chatting are especially handy when you travel.

Just remember to always take utmost care in this area. If your kids have access to your phone, you may end up answering some interesting questions. I've personally witnessed a few unfortunate mishaps where personal photos were accidentally shared on social media. When you're turned on, you can sometimes forget important details and make mistakes, so sext responsibly, my friends.

One very important thing to mention at this point is that if you're exchanging images of each other in order to excite yourselves, no images of other people should ever join the picture. More specifically: **Pornography is never a fruitful or healthy method of building intimacy with your spouse.**

Using the image of another person for sexual arousal is absolutely outside the healthy boundaries of marriage. If you use pornography in an attempt to spice things up or bring fulfillment to the bedroom, not only will this lead to unhealthy views about what sexual intimacy is, but it also means that your mind is engaging in sexual expression outside of your own marriage. This is certainly not in God's plan.

Allowing yourself or your spouse to become aroused at the image of another person is a form of infidelity, even if you're both in agreement on using it as a tool. (We'll talk more about pornography in Chapter Five.)

Whatever tool you may use, it's so important to make sure that it's never more than just a tool. It should never be an idol that takes the place of God or your husband in the bedroom, and it should never be a crutch that allows you to stop working in areas where you need to grow and strengthen your connection. If you're insisting on using your vibrator on yourself every time you get into bed, or if you're on the computer every night obsessing over finding the perfect sex lube and ignoring your husband's advances, you're missing the point. Base every single thing you do on the goal of connection.

God's Best for Your Sexy Self

You may have grown up as I did, in an environment where sex was not spoken about in a positive light, if at all. This may have given you a negative and unhealthy perspective of your sex drive. And as we've covered, this kind of miseducation can so easily lead to patterns of shame and isolation, especially when masturbation is thrown into the mix. The Lord is waiting to meet you in any area of your life where you've experienced lack, abuse, rebellion, or sadness. It's so important to understand that God's desire is for you to be liberated from any and all sexual bondage.

No matter where you're at, whether you're single or married, your fresh start can begin today. True repentance means changing your course and asking the Lord to guide you back onto His path. If it truly comes from your heart, even a simple prayer can change years of misguided anguish and give you a clean slate. If anything I've covered so far weighs on your heart, here's a simple prayer you can speak to the Lord:

Jesus, I come to you with a heart that wants to do your will in my life. Please forgive me for attempting to meet my sexual needs on my own, and for any sexual activity that was outside of your boundaries. I now see your desire for me to express my sexuality in a healthy way that serves a greater purpose: to strengthen intimacy with the husband you've chosen for me. Please guide me in managing my needs. I give you permission to address these unhealthy patterns in my life and I accept not only your forgiveness but the power you've given me to walk in sexual wholeness. I also invite you to strengthen my sex drive and guide it to your perfect purposes. Thank you for caring so deeply about these areas of my life. Thank you for being a wonderful father who patiently and lovingly desires to speak to me and teach me about my sexual desires. I receive your help and give you all of my heart. Amen.

Chapter Four

Fantasy: Healthy or Harmful?

*"Sex is perhaps eighty percent fantasy (imagination and mind)
and about twenty percent friction."*

—Dr. Douglas E Rosenau

The Importance of Our Imagination

As we talked about in the previous chapter, God designed us to respond sexually to physical stimulation; specific responses to specific stimulation results in sexual pleasure. Another important component that I mentioned was that the brain is the biggest sexual organ. For that reason, we are called not only to cultivate sexual liberty by understanding our *physical* makeup as women, but also by understanding our *minds*.

God designed our ability to imagine, and He gave this ability to us for a purpose. The New Testament in particular has a lot to say on the subject of imagination, or "seeing with the mind." And scripture clearly explains how our imaginations, and what we choose to dwell on in life, can bring us either great strength or great weakness. If we call ourselves stupid and weak, we will act in that manner; if we call ourselves brilliant and strong, that's what we'll be. Call the Bible old fashioned, but quantum physicists and the writers of loads of secular self-help books currently preach what the Bible's been telling us for thousands of years.

We humans tend to think in pictures, though we know from the Bible that we're capable of seeing with both our minds *and* our hearts (Ephesians 1:18). The heart, obviously, is the deepest place within us. This ability to see with both heart and mind is the bedrock on which our beliefs and faith rest. As Romans 10:17 says, *"So faith comes from hearing, and hearing through the word of Christ"* (ESV). When we first hear, and the Holy Spirit begins to work in our hearts, we "see." Our spiritual eyes open, we see our need for Him, and we no longer see ourselves from our own perspective. In our minds, we now see from His perspective. Our faith and beliefs become the foundation of our actions.

According to Merriam Webster's dictionary, *imagination* is defined as, "the act or power of forming a mental image of something not present to the senses or never before wholly perceived in reality." Our thoughts are where our faith in Jesus Christ originates and takes root in our lives. This explains the Bible's repeated call to guard our thoughts and to renew our minds. We have a mandate from the Lord to steward our imagination with His help. This means we are not victims to our imaginations, and that we have the power and authority in Christ to set our minds on godly things. As the Apostle Paul instructed us, *"Set your minds on things that are above, not on things that are on earth"* (Colossians 3:2 ESV).

The sanctified imagination is one that's focused upon the realities of heaven. Heaven is not just an idea or abstract concept, but it's an *actual place*, a *reality*; that's how Paul approached the subject of heaven. We're seated in heaven now, even though we're still in the earthly realm, and our "heart's eye" (imagination) is the way that we see beyond the natural decay of the physical world and stay connected to this heavenly reality. Hence, the need for us to always focus our internal vision on heaven.

This reminds me of the saying, "We're not earthly creatures who have spiritual experiences; we're spiritual creatures having an earthly experience." Our faith is grounded in our ability to imagine the promises of God, to rightly see His nature, and to walk according to His proclamations for this life. When you receive Christ as your Savior, you're called to a life of faith as Second Corinthians 5:7 declares: *"for we walk by faith, not by sight"* (ESV). This doesn't mean we walk around blind to things that we see in the world around us. No, this means that faith is our navigator. On a ship, the navigator tells the helmsman where to steer, but if it comes down to it, it's still the helmsman's responsibility to steer clear of any rocks.

We may think faith is tied to our imagination, but it goes beyond that and *permeates* our imagination. Our imagination is the starting point from which we choose to walk out our life and faith. Our imagination dwells in our mind, is accepted by our heart, and steers our body. Our mind, heart, and body are all connected, and our imagination directly affects our actions and what we believe about God and the world He created.

Now faith is the assurance of things hoped for, the conviction of things not seen. (Hebrews 11:1 ESV)

We all establish patterns in our imaginations; we all have different strengths when it comes to how we receive, process, access, and articulate information. These differences can impact both our natural and spiritual lives in different ways. Memories from the past, factual information from the here and now, and ideas and thoughts pertaining to the future are a powerful part of our lives, essential to our faith, and absolutely vital in living a life of freedom and abundance.

So, knowing all this, it's important to ask:

How do you see yourself?

How do you see Him?

How do you see your future?

The answers to these questions lie within the current state of your imagination. What you dwell on and allow to shape your imagination directly affects your walk of faith. Your walk of faith directly affects your relationship with God and others. A sanctified imagination has the power to receive inspiration from God and bring life to ourselves and those around us. Our mind's eye can be a steaming garbage dump of despair, or a shining tower of heavenly possibility.

Different Influences on Your Imagination

Your imagination can be influenced by different things, like your mental habits, surroundings, God, and the enemy. It's vital in your walk with the Lord to understand that not everything that pops into your head is your own thought, nor does it stem from your own identity.

The enemy watches your life like a hunter with a drawn arrow, waiting for just the right moment to hit your vulnerable areas and cripple you. He understands fully the power of your imagination and knows that what you believe will influence your behavior as well as your desire and ability to destroy his works.

In all circumstances take up the shield of faith, with which you can extinguish all the flaming darts of the evil one; and take the helmet of salvation, and the sword of the Spirit, which is the word of God...(Ephesians 6:16-17 ESV)

Understanding and meditating on what the Word of God says about us while spending time connecting with the Holy Spirit is how we shield ourselves from the darts of the enemy. This cultivates faith, and faith is our shield against the suggestions of the enemy that act against our mind and heart. And these darts will always be aimed at the areas of our lives that are lacking in faith—where we say we believe God, but our actions don't line up with that belief.

Yes, we were made with many vulnerabilities, and it can be easy to feel some resentment about it, but remember that we were made with vulnerabilities because we were made for dependence upon a God that protects us. We can protect ourselves with faith and by meditating on godly thoughts, but can be exposed to attacks from the enemy if we're not in a relationship with God. That's because we were created to walk with Him in the Garden! Our need for Him makes us beautiful! Callousness and misguided independence darken our minds and cause us to lose our authority over the enemy.

This has all been fairly general advice, but let's get back to the heart of the matter. Sometimes the attacks on our minds and imaginations are sexual in nature. This can be confusing, because sewing confusion is exactly how the enemy attacks us. However, as we've established, sexual thoughts are not sinful if they're within the boundaries that God has placed in our lives. I've met women who were married, yet still avoided any thoughts of sex and even the state of arousal. But sexual arousal is *amoral* because our bodies were designed by God to react in certain ways to stimulation and imagination. It only becomes *immoral* if our focus is on the wrong thing. For this one reason, imagination plays such a key role in our sex lives; it's the epicenter from which the morality of sex is decided. This is why the Bible speaks so frequently about what we choose to think and dwell on. Thinking about sex is not wrong. Thinking about sex in an *unhealthy* way is wrong and leads to bondage. But let's explore this topic in more detail.

Fantasy

Imagination involves picturing things that have happened and things that could take place. *Fantasy* is a closely related concept that Merriam Webster defines as "the power or process of creating especially unrealistic or improbable mental images." Fantasy is an aspect of our imagination that creates scenarios we wish were real. That's what makes fantasy so appealing. We're naturally fantastical creatures, and fantasy has contributed to many of the most creative and beautiful things in human history: stories, theater, dance, art, etc. However, the thing about fantasy is that a lot rides on its content.

What I fantasize about fills my heart. What fills my heart will manifest in the steps I take in my life. Does that mean fantasy is a sin? Absolutely not. Fantasy is yet another gift from God that needs to be kept under His guidance, influence, and authority, just like imagination, sex, and masturbation. These are all morally neutral but need to be stewarded so that they don't bind us to sinful patterns.

Finally, brethren, whatever things are true, whatever things are noble, whatever things are just, whatever things are pure, whatever things are lovely, whatever things are of good report, if there is any virtue and if there is anything praiseworthy—meditate on these things. (Philippians 4:8 NKJV)

What we dwell on is what we worship. We're either enjoying an exciting and hopeful imagination where God is allowed to guide and inspire us, or we're partnering with images, thoughts, and content that is self-serving and ungodly. There are many self-serving and self-exalting images that lead to sin. How do we know the difference between a good thought and a bad one?

God defines what is good. Jesus is our example. Are our fantasies filled with self-serving ideas and motives, or are they filled with the possibility of self-sacrificial love that focuses on other people in a way that establishes the kingdom of God? Our definition of what's good definitely can't be based on our own emotions; just because something invokes a feeling that we subjectively perceive as good doesn't mean we should accept it. To use a similar analogy to the one earlier, Satan always has a fishing line all hooked and baited and ready for us, if we're willing to bite. Too often the bait is something that looks good, and we don't realize we have just been snagged by the hook of compromise.

Early Encounters with the Power of Fantasy

My earliest memory of a vivid, full-color fantasy dates back to the playground when I was six. My heart was going pitter patter for a blue-eyed, blonde-haired Brad Pitt look-alike in my kindergarten. His name was *Hugh…* The name was like flower petals on the wind. One day, I found myself watching him from a comfortable distance on the playground and drifting into my very first fantasy.

In this fantasy, Hugh was in distress. Even though Hugh was naturally superb at climbing monkey bars and jumping from the swings with that devil-may-care attitude I so admired, he was now trapped on top of the swing set. See, Hugh had climbed the metal frame to safety because the ground below, once covered in nothing but pea gravel and empty juice boxes, was now *swarming with man-eating alligators!* Oh, but these were no ordinary, run-of-the-mill playground alligators. These were neon purple, and they had red laser eyes!

Driven by my burning affection, naturally, I leapt into action. I grabbed one of the vines that were suddenly and very conveniently placed all over the playground and swung toward him. I made my way to the swing set, and with one hand I was able to snatch up my darling in distress just before the alligators could bite our dangling feet. Indeed, if it weren't for me, Hugh would have been gator food.

Good work, six-year-old Liz.

Suffice it to say, a rush of dopamine hit my little brain and euphoria followed. I remember lying in the grass beside the playground, basking in the sun and in my mental achievements. All at once, I had discovered the power of fantasy, and paint me green and call me a cucumber, I was hooked! My little mental escapade created a real, physical reaction in my body. Even though this wasn't sexual in any way, it was still an *emotional* rush—and one that was not rooted in reality.

In reality, I was a very shy little girl and on the heavier side, so Hugh didn't chase me or show any signs of interest like he did with the other girls. Without psychoanalyzing myself too deeply, I would say I was attempting to navigate my real desire for connection through imaginings in which I was not only emotionally connected, but a heroine. Unfortunately, I couldn't have known then that this would turn into a pattern that would lead to much dysfunction in my life.

My ability to create a vibrant fantasy, rich with color and intrigue, was a gift from God. I can't stress enough that fantasy is not a sin, but developing a pattern of fantasy that involves other people in situations that are too far removed from reality—as I did at this young age—opens the door to an overall unhealthy thought life. This leads to deeper feelings of isolation and depression. Naturally these feelings just make you want to indulge in fantasy even *more*, and before you know it, you're caught in a vicious cycle.

When you spend time fantasizing about unrealistic scenarios with other people, you set yourself up for further pain. You become disheartened by the expectations another person is not fulfilling because you've taken license in a relationship that hasn't naturally developed to that point. In other words, I forced Hugh to play into my fantasy life even though there was no evidence that he wanted to play into my *real* life. He might have avoided me on the playground, but in my mind, he had no say in the matter. This is how fantasy is like a drug; it feels great in the moment, but it always leaves you feeling even more empty and hurt after you engage with it.

As time passed and I made my way through my elementary years, fantasy was my constant companion. It was my means of escape whenever rejection and pain reared their ugly heads. Most nights I would want to retire to my room early, so I could lie in bed and recount the events of my day—only with different, more exciting outcomes. If I had an argument with somebody, I would go back and blast that person with all the things I couldn't articulate the first time around. If I had embarrassed myself by incorrectly answering one of my teacher's questions in front of the class, I would go back and nail the question with confidence, beaming under the gaze of my impressed classmates. If the boys had teased me about my weight, I would dream that instead they'd flirted with me and passed me notes that read, "Do you like me?" with checkboxes for "yes" and "no," and of course they would be on the edge of their seats as they watched me ponder their notes, trying to decide if I was feeling generous that day. (And as you can imagine, an overweight, lovesick girl's fantasies contain a fair amount of revenge scenarios as well.)

Not all of my fantasies were unhealthy. Sometimes they were the kind of stuff any little girl would daydream about—riding unicorns through enchanted forests, having superpowers, becoming a stand-up comedian. These daydreams were creative and adventurous. These were fantasies that, if nurtured and brought before the Lord, could have deepened my understanding of the creative gift He gave me.

Perhaps I could have been led to write stories, or paint what I saw in my mind, or audition for school plays. This could have been a great avenue of creativity, but instead of using my gift to liberate and expand myself, I wrangled it into protecting me from pain. Instead of giving this more creative part of my brain the attention it needed, I let my schoolyard fantasies take up most of the real estate in my mind. This was the shaky foundation of my emotional development that left me vulnerable and open to even more pain down the line.

As I hit puberty and my sex drive began to rear its ugly head, my habit of escaping into fantasy naturally transitioned into a habit of masturbating. I thought my elementary years were awkward? How does B.O., hormones, clumsiness and an even a bigger gut sound? Middle school only intensified my need for escape and brought my fantasy life to a whole new level. And when sex entered the mix, my imagination became more distorted than ever. This thing that was designed to breathe life into my relationship with God and keep me from isolation instead entrapped me. **My gift developed into bondage because I had not invited God to guide my thought life.**

I gave away my God-given authority in exchange for a false sense of power over my life. In my own fantasy world, I controlled all people and all outcomes. My wildest fantasies came true every day. Meditating on these fantasies—sexual or not—halted all growth that God wanted to see within me. I never needed to grow my relationships or solve my problems or take risks when I only had to plop down on my bed and retreat to my happy place at the end of the day.

Fantasy and the Single Life

Let's imagine, if you will, that you are a single woman working on a crab fishing boat in Alaska. You're one woman, on an otherwise all-male boat, in an industry dominated by men. Your captain is a stern man who keeps to himself when he isn't barking orders at his crew. You keep your head down and concentrate on your smelly job, stuffing ground-up squid and sardines into a bait sack.

One day, after sixteen nonstop hours of grueling labor, with cramped hands and blisters the size of tomatoes, you sit down to eat with the crew. The captain eats his dinner without so much as looking your way, only giving his attention to the men. You're exhausted and hurt. All you want is a little recognition for keeping up the work pace. The next morning, you start the excruciating day all over again. As you rip the guts out of a sardine, you find yourself in a daydream…

The captain emerges from his cabin. He limps over to you with his one wooden leg (did I mention he had a wooden leg?), peering down at you with his one eye (the other has a black patch), and says in his gruff voice, "Lovely and fair one, you be the best bait-bagger in all the sea." He brushes your hair away from your fish-splattered face and walks back to the wheelhouse, leaving you to bask in the glorious glow of affirmation.

How or why this guy turned into a pirate, I don't know. But I think you get the point; fantasy is an alternate reality in which we can meet our unmet, *legitimate* emotional needs.

You have legitimate needs. God created you to respond to godly and human affirmation. If you spend your time living in a fantasy world, there is no room for God to bring *His* affirmation. Under ideal circumstances, yes, God wants you to be affirmed and valued by those around you. As you well know, however, there are many times that does not happen, and we have to learn to navigate those places of disappointment where people let us down.

If you're like the woman on that crab fishing boat, and you're keeping yourself busy fantasizing about the captain in your life, it could mean two things. First, you're not dialoguing with God about what's going on, and as a result you're missing an important moment of intimacy with Him. He's a wonderful Father who wants to express His love. Second, you're putting unrealistic expectations on someone, which will strain an already difficult relationship. In trying to quell your hunger for affirmation by imaginary means, you ultimately deepen your disappointment and very possibly hinder your ability to function. Instead of three ground squids in your bait sack, maybe you'll start only having time for two.

However, if you fully submit your thoughts to the Lord, not only do you get all the "attaboys" you need, but you also open yourself up to a very healthy kind of fantasy. When He is allowed to help meet those needs, you can turn your fulfillment fantasies into ones about fulfilling *other people's* needs. Daydreaming about ways to bless and encourage others is most certainly healthy! This is what the sanctified mind was designed for! In the fishing boat example, you could fantasize about ways to bless your captain and crew after taking the time to strengthen yourself in the Lord. If you dialogue with the Holy Spirit as you slop that squid into a bag, you may get a brilliant and innovative idea about streamlining the baiting process.

As silly as this crab fishing example may be, it illustrates that there are countless chances to fall into the fantasy trap in our everyday lives and relationships, especially if we're single—in the office, at home, or even at church. Walking out singleness with joy and a sound mind can be a long, challenging journey. Even if some of these solutions sound *simple*, that doesn't mean they're always easy. Sometimes the urge to fall back on old patterns of thinking can become very strong. This is why learning to discipline your mind with the Holy Spirit's guidance is crucial.

Your relationships are the training grounds where you prepare yourself to one day build a marriage and a family. And if you're choosing celibacy and don't wish to marry, these training grounds prepare you for future platonic relationships. No matter your calling, this is important, and it's important to remember that it's a learned skill. No one is born understanding how to manage their imaginations, nor are they born understanding how to manage their sex drives.

As we have a tendency to sexualize our needs, it's not a surprise that fantasies can become sexual very quickly. When we as single women have active sexual fantasy lives, we're more than likely connecting these fantasies to masturbation. If God intends for you to only be bonded with one man in marriage, then fantasizing about a person you aren't married to it opens your heart to a connection it was never meant to have. Why? Because you were made to be *pursued and valued.*

When you masturbate while fantasizing about someone, there is no reciprocation of love and intimacy. It perpetuates the cycle of self-centeredness—the cycle of trying to fulfill your own needs. Isolation and hopelessness inevitably settle in after your orgasm is over, instead of the sense of connection and satisfaction you would feel in the context of a healthy marriage. It robs you of the true comfort and legitimacy that the Holy Spirit desires to bring into your life.

I've received a lot of aid in living a fulfilling life by observing some of my single friends. These women face the temptation of sexual fantasy or of going beyond healthy boundaries while dating, just like anyone. Like mine, their sex drives are ever-present. However, they have an action plan, one where they are very intentional with their time, thoughts, and actions. They have healthy habits in place to achieve that fulfillment.

Here are a few things I've observed about these women:

1. They engage in social activities often. My single friends who steward their imaginations well tend to find it easier when they aren't alone most the time. Even if they're on the introverted side, they often go out with other single friends and choose activities that engage their minds.

2. They avoid certain media when they are feeling vulnerable. It isn't prudish legalism to avoid certain movies, books, and social media platforms when you know you're going through a weaker time in your life. This is wisdom. It's a plan to successfully guard your heart while you are strengthened by the Lord, and it doesn't have to be permanent.

3. They spend a lot of time getting involved in their communities. Some of them lead church groups, some work to bring solutions to their neighborhoods, some have returned to school, and so on. A place where you can serve others or work in a group can provide a healthy sense of belonging. When you're dreaming up ways to make your community better, you don't have as much time to spend fantasizing about the guy next door.

4. They are in a daily pursuit to discover more of God. When you see the Lord as one who wants to awaken everything that He created within you, and not a God that wants to take away liberties from you, you face a grand adventure. I have single friends who pray, "Lord, awaken me to all you have, and help me discover anything about you that I'm missing out on." Such a simple and vital prayer to keep your imagination active and attuned to the exciting things happening in the Kingdom of God.

Fantasy and the Married Woman

For married women, fantasy can be a tool used for intimacy with your spouse. Just as it is with masturbation, this doesn't give you a free pass to stuff yourself silly at The Buffet of Sexual Fantasies; dialoguing with the Holy Spirit is essential to make sure you stay within His healthy boundaries. Daydreaming about having sex with your husband is awesome, but if your thirty-something chunky husband suddenly has the body of the twenty-year-old firefighter you passed by on your way to work, things have fallen into unhealthy territory. Fantasy can involve a change in location, narrative or roles, but should never involve a change of person, be it you or your husband.

Fantasizing can be enjoyed alone or with your husband, and these boundaries stand in both cases. Verbalizing your fantasies to your husband so that he can join in your arousal is the one and only goal here; it builds strong communication and connectedness. Fantasy needs to always promote safe play and humor—never fear, coercion, or pressure. Healthy sexual fantasy never involves other people or harmful situations. Violence, control, manipulation, and other demeaning actions are not God's idea of mirroring the image of Christ and the Church.

There are many women who have overcome—or are currently overcoming—sexual abuse, and expressing any kind of sexual fantasy can be painful for them. It's very important that your husband is aware of your abuse, and it's equally important that he shows patience and understanding as you address it. In all of God's goodness, I do believe that full sexual freedom is available for everyone because of what Christ has provided for us. No one on Earth is hopeless in this regard, no one is beyond His help. And even further, you can come to enjoy your sex life just as much as anyone who has not been abused. Believe and ask for a complete and utter restoration... and then some! After all, we serve an abundant God.

It's important to remember that we need to use our imaginations responsibly, but it's also important to know that there's far more creativity available to us than we often realize. In the church, sex has historically been reduced to nothing more than duty, and most certainly not an expression of intimacy and ecstasy. This old-fashioned mindset is all-or-nothing, black-or-white. Sex and fantasy can lead to sin, so they get thrown out with the bathwater and stripped down to something that you either do without pleasure or you don't do at all. This mindset of course ignores and undermines our ability to gain wisdom through the Holy Spirit.

I know I've said it many times already, but it's just so important: **Open communication with the Holy Spirit is key when it comes to fantasy.** If what your mind lingers on has not creatively originated from the Holy Spirit, it can lead to distortion. It's especially important here to protect yourself and your marriage. Affairs begin by allowing yourself to entertain thoughts of another man playing the role your husband has been called to. These thoughts can erode your marriage.

Fortunately, we know that old-fashioned church ideology doesn't have all the right info. Just because fantasy can be misguided and abused doesn't mean we shouldn't engage in it. Fantasy is like a car; it has the potential to cause great damage, but it's a valuable asset when used correctly. Just learn to drive soberly and responsibly.

Play in Fantasy

Role-playing can be a lot of fun. Pretending you're an American Olympic swimmer and your husband is the British weightlifting champion that you just met at a celebratory party because you both won Gold Medals that day... Uh, that's just *one example* that *someone, somewhere* might use... Okay, this is totally me and my husband. The Sunday school girl part of me even threw in "and we find a pastor to marry us on sight before we get to the hotel" just to make it legal.

In this silly scenario, are we becoming aroused by the thought of being with different people, or by pretending that we're different people? Most definitely not. We're simply playing with scenarios and roles that are complete fabrications. We're not putting bags over our heads, so we can pretend to be others; at the core of this fantasy, we're still *us*. In fact, my husband loves weightlifting, and I love to swim, so a humorous scenario like this one is a way to acknowledge that we know each other well. It points to the fun and creative things we each know would light the other up. It's all about playing and discovering what makes our spouses tick.

Dialoguing about past experiences together is another way to bring healthy fantasy into your bedroom. Identifying something specific that your spouse once enjoyed makes for a great opportunity for connection. Let's say one year around Christmas time you had great sex by the Christmas tree while wrapping presents. So, the next year your husband surprises you with flowers by the wrapping paper, leading to a reenactment. This kind of gesture communicates that he's paying close attention to what you like and trying to foster pleasant memories between you. It's a relatively simple use of fantasy, but a powerful one. (For the record, this is not a personal example. Present wrapping for us usually means a mad dash to wrap everything two days before Christmas.)

Prayer

The idea that imagination is a gift may be new to you. Just know it's not by accident that you're reading this book today. God wants you free so that He can partner with you to fill your emotional needs. If you feel you have an out-of-control imagination and fantasy life that's not submitted to Him and you want freedom today, I invite you to pray this from the heart:

Jesus, thank you for giving me a mind with endless possibilities. I know that nothing is impossible when I come into agreement with your will for my life. Lord, forgive me for my misuse of my imagination and for not allowing you to speak to me in this area. I give you permission to meet me here and help me discern through the Holy Spirit's guidance when I'm going off track or thinking about things that hinder me from seeing your will. Please partner with me in my thought life so that I have your mind. I invite you now to cleanse me of every fantasy I've had outside of your boundaries. Please break the power of unholy fantasy over my life now. Thank you for restoring my imagination. Amen!

Some of you may need to get rid of books, movies, music, or other items that you use as a tool for fantasy. The Holy Spirit will increase your sensitivity to what you see, hear, and think about now that you have opened your heart to His ways for your life. But you might need to go further than this, because you may be one of the many women who have taken things further than just unhealthy thoughts and masturbation. For these women, pornography is an ever-present reality.

Chapter Five

Pornography

"*Learning how to bring our struggling to Christ's Cross is to recognize that there's nothing of your struggle that is unwelcome in Heaven or unwilling to be heard by the Father.*"

—Jack Hayford

Pornography: AKA Pandora's Glitter Box of Anguish

When the mind and emotions have few to no boundaries, a great vulnerability to sin is present. Cultivating a life of sexual fantasy and masturbation can easily open you up to using pornography.

Pornography, by definition, is the depiction of erotic behavior that is intended to cause sexual excitement. Over the years, pornography has taken many forms and, in fact, it's had a huge impact on many entertainment mediums. For older generations, magazines with nude photos were most common, whereas movies were harder to access. In the 80's and 90's, the invention of both VHS and cable made videos much more accessible. Now, with the Internet and smartphones, pornographic exposure can happen in an instant, even with the strongest filters possible on your computer. This is because the porn industry knows the power of the product they push. Whether it's magazines or 800 numbers or chat rooms or movies, pornography has evolved to find us where we are and made it easier and easier for us to chase our sexual fantasies.

What Pornography Does to the Brain

An orgasm is conditional. As we discussed in the masturbation chapter, when you stimulate nerve endings in the vagina and combine that with erotic images, an orgasm can occur. Then, as we talked about in the section on sex before marriage, orgasms release chemicals in the brain. Two of these are oxytocin and dopamine.

Oxytocin is one of the reasons we tend to feel isolation and sadness after masturbating alone. If you reach orgasm and your brain tells you to bond with your partner, the experience can feel very empty and wrong if you're alone.

Dopamine is the big one, though. Dopamine is released during sex and sends rewarding signals to your brain by affecting its pleasure center. Your brain is wired to tell you, "Good job having sex. You should do that again." After dopamine is released, it alters your brain cells to promote certain actions and creates a path that strengthens the power of the reward. Eventually your brain begins to release dopamine when it even *predicts* that sex is coming. This process actually happens in any area of your life where you experience the reward of pleasure, whether it's sex, a good meal, or playing a game of tennis.

If I learn to associate the Chick-fil-A drive through with the pleasure explosion of a Dreamsicle ice cream cone, then my dopamine levels increase as I turn the corner and enter the line to place my order. This connection is then reinforced if I eat the delicious vanilla ice cream with sprinkles on top (another one of God's divine creations). However, if I pull out of the drive through with a salad, the dopamine release is decreased, and the connection is weakened. (A side note: I've shed over a hundred pounds as of this writing by learning to associate reward with healthy foods as a primary tool to create new pathways in my brain.)

Again, dopamine release is a conditioned action. If you've learned to associate your husband's touch with an orgasm, then dopamine will be released when he touches you and you'll be stimulated as a result. This is important because it helps us understand how easy it is to get trapped in patterns of sexual brokenness, and it's also key in understanding how to break these patterns. You can create healthy dopamine release patterns, or you can create unhealthy ones. What you think about and reinforce with action not only becomes habit, but it also creates real, physical markers in your brain.

The cycle of being porn dependent contains several steps. It doesn't happen overnight or with one usage. The more you engage with pornography, the stronger the dependency becomes.

1. First you are exposed to pornography and begin to **build up a tolerance to it**. What took you five minutes to bring you to orgasm now takes twenty minutes. What you watched before is not enough. There are many reasons for this, but one has to do with our bodies not being made for such a frequent amount of intense stimulus. Over time, this high level of stimulus creates a desensitivity in both the body and the mind. The more you learn about sex, the more you see that sensitivity is important for a successful orgasm; but this sensitivity is naturally dulled when you come at it with a

fire hose of illicit sexual content and stimulation. It isn't the fact that you're having frequent orgasms that desensitizes you; it's the way in which you're engaging your brain to achieve those orgasms.

2. After becoming desensitized you start to develop **obsessive behaviors**. You frequently think about the next time you can watch porn. You strategize the time and place of your next consumption of it, so no one will know. Your brain wants nothing more than to get that sweet dopamine release. At this time, it's easy to fall into the trap of believing that maybe God is actually okay with you viewing porn.

3. You begin to **lose control** and your viewing of porn **becomes compulsive**. I'm not saying that you become a monster and begin storming the streets like the Hulk, grunting, "Me need porn! Me need porn!" or breaking into adult stores and stealing porn at gunpoint. Not quite that far. But it does start to interrupt your life, and you find yourself driving home on your lunch break to watch it. Maybe you start to distance yourself from God and others. Plans are changed, and trips are canceled when you find that you're afraid of going without it for too long.

4. Lastly, you **experience withdrawals** when you go without porn. You're moody, lonely, depressed, irritable, and so on when you go too long without being able to watch it. As a note, even when you're not viewing porn but are still utilizing the images during masturbation, the strong oxytocin and dopamine releases are still taking place, thus continuing the cycle.

Your porn addiction may look a little different from mine, and you may go through seasons where you're viewing less, but this is the general process it takes us through. This is the result of a constant abuse of our hormonal releases.

God designed this powerful system of hormones so that we could experience unmatched physical rewards for connecting in our healthy marriages. It's kind of like God strung a carrot on a stick in front of a rabbit, then gave the rabbit the stick. Instead of something to simply indulge in, it's a motivator. Within the context of marriage, God wants you to associate sex with reward. This reward is for building a strong and bonded sex life with your spouse. It's the reward for sacrificing for each other, learning about each other, and preferring each other in love.

Christian Women and Pornography

Christian women are not immune to the draw of pornography. In fact, I believe that Christian women are not accurately represented in the statistics gathered about pornography usage because of the nature of our church culture surrounding women and sexuality. If women don't feel safe sharing that kind of information with their Christian community to get help, they probably don't feel safe sharing it with a poll.

Pornography usage in our secular culture seems to be so common among men that it's almost *expected*. As such, there are some churches that provide resources for men who want help with their pornography usage. Because of the taboo nature of female sexuality, however, such resources for women are few and far between. This is sad, because any believer can be bound by sin. *Anyone* can be saved, yet not experience the kingdom of God because of that bondage. These kinds of sexual issues apply to both men and women, especially in an age where our culture wants to define our morality without examining the costs.

What Scripture Says About Pornography

Scripture is clear when it comes to pornography. From a biblical perspective, there's no question that using pornography is not

God's will for your life. Pornography is sin and it damages our ability to live healthy lives. It's a counterfeit version of sexual fulfillment and intimacy. And like I explained in the previous chapter, all sex (including sexual arousal) outside of marriage is outside of God's plan.

> *Put to death therefore what is earthly in you: sexual immorality, impurity, passion, evil desire, and covetousness, which is idolatry.* (Colossians 3:5 ESV)

> *Now the works of the flesh are evident, which are: adultery, fornication, uncleanness, lewdness, idolatry, sorcery, hatred, contentions, jealousies, outbursts of wrath, selfish ambitions, dissensions, heresies, envy, murders, drunkenness, revelries, and the like; of which I tell you beforehand, just as I also told you in time past, that those who practice such things will not inherit the kingdom of God.* (Galatians 5:19-21 NKJV)

> *But fornication and all uncleanness or covetousness, let it not even be named among you, as is fitting for saints; neither filthiness, nor foolish talking, nor coarse jesting, which are not fitting, but rather giving of thanks.*
> (Ephesians 5:3-4 NKJV)

> *But I say to you that whoever looks at a woman to lust for her has already committed adultery with her in his heart.*
> (Matthew 5:28 NKJV)

The word "fornication" present in all of the scriptures listed above is translated from the Greek word "porneia," from which we get the word pornography. Porneia is defined as illicit sexual intercourse or even as idol worship. Porneia is sexual immorality, which is defined as all sex outside of the covenant of marriage. Pornography involves other people, plain and simple. You are being stimulated by images of other people having sex. This is fornication and warned about as sin in many passages of scripture.

Throughout the Bible, sex outside of marriage is tied to idolatry. Why is this? Because Jesus loves His people (the church) as a husband loves his wife; His relationship with us mirrors monogamy. Anything you introduce into your life in order to find meaning, belonging, and fulfillment becomes a "god," and worshiping one of these idols obviously does not reflect God's nature.

Can you love Jesus and still watch pornography? Yes. You can always have faith in Jesus, absolutely. However, every time you allow another god to influence you, you harm yourself and further distance yourself from the truth of the gospel. You come to the table of freedom and refuse to eat. You don't receive the gift of redemption from sin that Jesus paid for through His death and resurrection. Jesus requires that we lay down our lives for His truth. When you say you love Him but are far from truly knowing Him, then you're not loving Him with all of your heart. You inherit the kingdom of the god you give your heart to, whether that's the One True God, or a porn site you visit every day.

It's incredibly important to see how this sin robs you of your freedom and causes harm to your body and mind. Sin is what Satan introduced into The Garden, from outside of God's paradise. We want to return to The Garden and live in our creator's presence without being pulled away by any hooks sin might have in us. This requires that we understand sin clearly.

My Story

As I discussed in my book *The God of My Parents: The Uncensored Account of My Journey to Find Identity*, pornography played a huge role in my sexual development growing up. I was first exposed to pornography in elementary school. While visiting a friend after school one day, I stumbled across pornography in her bathroom. Curiosity led me to open that copy of Playboy, and it felt like I had stumbled upon something magical. After I went home and came down from the "high," however, I was hit by a wave of shame. Like I said before, with my mother's history of sexual abuse and our family's "traditional" mindset when it came to sex, this was not an experience I felt I could share with my parents. I kept it hidden away and it wasn't long before I sought out this magical new thing myself.

With my already active fantasy life and my struggles with rejection and anxiety, pornography provided me with instant relief and false gratification. No longer did I have to imagine sexual interactions in order to become aroused; porn was a direct line to my heart, mind, and body. No longer did I have to be confused or go without comfort; the education, conversation, and stimulation I so desperately craved was now right in front of me. Porn was there for me.

My relationship with pornography was eventually coupled with masturbation and a cycle of seeking out more and more pornography, all while still hiding everything from my parents. In high school our family upgraded to satellite TV. Before that we had a whopping four channels, so naturally this was very exciting. Most exciting of all though, some channels showed soft porn after a certain time at night. I had a TV in my room. You can imagine how that turned out. My parents continued to avoid talking about that aspect of my life, and I continued to reap the "rewards" of their hands-off parenting.

When I reached college, things naturally escalated to a whole new level. I mean, I was finally an adult with my own money, a car, an apartment, access to adult stores, and no one to report to. These were the porn-viewing big leagues! Then, of course, it didn't take long before I breached that final frontier: sexual experiences with other people.

This, by my own definition at the time, should have been the pinnacle of my sexual freedom and expression. However, it was actually dehumanizing and deprived me of any sort of peace or happiness. The further I went down that magical rabbit hole, the more lost and miserable I felt.

One night I had an encounter with God and returned to the Lord. I moved to a new city and began attending ministry school. And that's the end of my story, right? Everything was perfect after that?

Wish I could say it was. Even while attending a school of ministry, I continued to be bound by patterns of pornography usage and fantasy. The only difference was that I felt infinitely more shame for it. Even after returning to the Lord, I still didn't know how to break the cycle, and I didn't believe that I would ever be free from pornography. It wasn't until I found a ministry that focused specifically on sexual brokenness that I received the tools I needed to be free.

My story is irrefutable proof that **you can be bound by sexual addiction and find complete freedom**. It's not just wishful thinking, and it's not a magical happily ever after fairytale that's beyond your grasp. Every believer is given access to this freedom through Jesus' death and resurrection. As I'll discuss in the next chapter, the key to this freedom is dependent on you giving God and others access to your brokenness.

Pornography and the Single Woman

As a single Christian woman, you are just as susceptible to the trap of pornography as men are. Many single women use pornography as an aid in walking out their celibacy as they wait to find a husband. As I hope you can see, this is not a healthy means for you to steward your sex drive. In fact, your usage of pornography can be hindering your progress in finding the spouse God has for you. Addressing these issues now so that you don't gravitate toward men with the same issues is also important.

Pornography

Single women may use pornography for different reasons, but the most common one seems to be a craving for comfort and excitement, as was the case with me. When you're single and living alone, it can be difficult to break free from pornography because of the easy accessibility to porn and the smaller chance of being "caught." It's also hard when you're single because there isn't as much motivation to change compared to someone who's married. The cost of your pornography usage isn't felt as strongly because (at least at first glance) it looks like you're only hurting yourself. When you live alone, no partner or children are being affected by your behavior.

For the single woman, breaking free from the cycle begins with your identity in God, through which you'll realize that your actions do affect the lives of others. Addiction issues like this can keep others from knowing the true you that's hiding behind pornography. The world needs you present and healthy! You are a gift!

Pornography and the Married Woman

When you're married and consuming pornography, the dynamics are somewhat different. The main reason is the effect your usage has on your family. The constant need to keep things out of the light creates a very damaging and guarded environment. You provide a spiritual covering for your home and what you do sets the tone for the rest of the house.

When you allow your porn usage to remain both active and hidden, the effects on your marriage are many. First, you withdraw from God and your heart becomes callous in many ways. What once moved you now doesn't affect you. Your response to His caring convictions lessens. Barricades go up around your heart and you're not able to fully receive the strength from the Lord that you need to thrive in a healthy family.

Second, you erode your ability to have an intimate relationship with your husband without aid of pornographic imagery—live or through memories. Earlier we talked about desensitization and it's more obvious than ever when you're in the bedroom; if you commonly look to perfect sexual idols for your burst of dopamine, how is your husband going to compare? And if you're conjuring up images of another man or woman while being physically intimate with your husband, that is not building intimacy with him; that is *using him as an object* for your own stimulation. This is exactly opposite to how God designed sex, and it's what the Bible defines as both idolatry and adultery—idolatry because you're uniting with false images and worshiping false gods, and adultery because you're arousing yourself using the image of a man you're not married to.

Only your husband is fitted for that place in your life. Bringing others into your thoughts pollutes that idea of marriage as a representation of Christ and the church. Spiritually you're outside of God's design, emotionally your relationship suffers, and physically you create a pattern wherein your spouse is no longer enough to arouse you. You train your brain to become non-responsive to the image of your hot, naked husband and that's going to bring a lot of pain to your marriage. You were never made for this. You were made to reflect and honor God with your body and soul.

Thinking that it's beneficial to use pornography mutually as a sex aid when you're married is common in this day and age, but it's still very misguided for the reasons I've already listed. Even if all you're doing is trying to make the experience better for both parties, this makes sex all about the orgasm when it's supposed to be about nurturing and caring for each other. My husband and I work with many couples who suffer under the effects of bringing pornography into their marriage thinking it would benefit them, and we've seen firsthand that it only adds disconnect, pain, and distortion to their sexual union.

I'm a strong believer that every married woman should know how to achieve orgasm with her husband during sex. (Once again, you don't have to orgasm every time you have sex, but being an empowered woman means you understand what feels good to you.) If you struggle in this area, there are many tools and godly methods to turn to besides pornography. Self-exploration is very helpful, as we talked about earlier, but another good tool is seeing a marriage counselor or a trusted pastor who's not afraid to talk about sex.

Bring God into the issue. Sometimes when you try to fix your own problems in your own way, you can damage or even break the very thing you're trying to save. Live in clear view of His best and believe in His ability to help you, even if it feels like your circumstances are warring against you.

Just remember that an orgasm is not a badge of success; it's a vehicle for intimacy. There are couples for whom erectile dysfunction or medical issues prevent "sex as usual," and they nevertheless find ways to stay sexually connected.

Lastly, if your husband has pressured you into using pornography with him, there is nothing in God's word that says you're required to continue doing so. In fact, purposefully stepping out of a sinful pattern will hopefully set an example for your husband and enable God to reach him. This is true for any illicit behavior; if you're feeling pressure to do anything that makes you uncomfortable (especially if it can be considered abusive) stop taking part, establish healthy boundaries, and even consider seeking a counselor for help.

Even if you stumbled into something like this with complete willingness, there is no obligation to continue in order to appease your husband. Following your husband into sexual brokenness won't build anything but dysfunction.

Discover Eden

Get Rid of the Crap and You Get Rid of the Flies

Renew your mind and these unhealthy patterns will be broken. You can be free *today* from pornography and any other spiritual doors you've opened through your usage. Just understand that the root issue of sexual brokenness is always relational. You'll need to ditch lies you've believed about God and yourself, learn new patterns of behavior, learn to partner with the Holy Spirit in all areas of your life, and renew your mind daily with God's word. It's not a perfect, instant fix, and those temptation hooks may keep trying to find you for a time, but freedom is always waiting for you. You can stop watching pornography today.

When an unclean spirit goes out of a man, he goes through dry places, seeking rest; and finding none, he says, 'I will return to my house from which I came.' And when he comes, he finds it swept and put in order. Then he goes and takes with him seven other spirits more wicked than himself, and they enter and dwell there; and the last state of that man is worse than the first. (Luke 11:24-26 NKJV)

In these verses, Jesus explains to the Pharisees His power over evil forces and the responsibility of believers once He frees them and commands them to go. Throughout the New Testament, Jesus tries to get it through the Pharisees' heads that He is the Messiah and they are hypocrites. They "know" the Word of God but fail miserably to understand it because they don't truly know God. The Pharisees base their righteousness on appearance, religious rituals, and title.

In Luke 11, Jesus describes the condition of a person who simply plays by surfacey, shallow religious rules without Christ. In this scripture, the house represents the man's life. Outwardly, everything seems put together, he looks tidy, the floor is swept, and he owns

111

some furniture. This is akin to saying and doing the things you're expected to say and do because you're more concerned about your appearance than you are about relationships.

There was a time when I was a master at this and that's why I struggled so much with my faith. Outwardly, I learned to give people what they wanted. As was the case with the man in Luke 11, this opened the door to many nasty things. And eventually, when I had bankrupted my religious bank and was forced to face my pain and trauma, I finally stopped trying to keep the surface clean. I stopped sweeping and let the mess come through.

Neutrality is not an option in the gospel. You're either submitted to Him or not. Do we go through hard times that test our faith? Absolutely. There is a big difference, however, between leaning on Jesus when you're feeling weak and frantically grasping for relief in harmful ways while avoiding Him because your perception of Him is wrong.

Most of the years I struggled with sexual brokenness, I was rebelling against my false view of God and against religion as a whole. My understanding of Him was surfacey and immature. My pride kept me from a lot of wonderful things He had for me during those years. If I knew Him then like I know Him now, I don't believe I would have had the urge to self-destruct as I did. The kicker here is that you have to humble yourself to see Him clearly, to trust and have faith in something that's bigger than you and beyond your control. That might not be easy to do when you're not seeing Jesus clearly and you're allowing life circumstances and the lies of the enemy to define God instead of letting Him define Himself. In order to truly know Him, you need to humble yourself and ask for help.

God doesn't require humility because He's a controlling dictator. He requires humility because He is humble. You won't begin to understand His kindness and His nature until you drop the prideful idea that you have everything together and figured out. It's possible to read the Bible a hundred times over and still not truly know His heart for you. God ultimately wants you to reflect His humble nature because you were made in His image, and being humble means asking for help.

Prayer, Repentance, and Renouncement

If you're stuck in a cycle of using pornography then get ready, because Jesus is going to set you free today! Pray this prayer with me and ask Him to lay out the next steps in your plan of action. Then in the next chapter we'll talk about steps to staying free.

Jesus, thank you for never giving up on me. Thank you for pursuing me and remaining faithful to me even when I am not faithful to you. I see how damaging and dehumanizing pornography is now and I want to end my relationship with it today. Holy Spirit, I invite you to break all bonds on my body and soul that were created by my usage. I invite you to speak to me clearly about this pattern in my life. Thank you for giving me the power to break this pattern by the blood of Jesus. Jesus, forgive me for polluting my sexuality with other people and images that are not of you. I receive your forgiveness today and fully expect you to guide me into wholeness. Thank you for being a loving God who desires nothing more than my freedom. I receive it today. Amen!

Chapter Six

Breaking Free
The New Creation Mindset

"If you believe you will not be free from sin until you die, you have just made death your savior instead of Jesus."

—Bill Johnson

Am I an addict?

But God demonstrates His own love toward us, in that while we were still sinners, Christ died for us. (Romans 5:8 NKJV)

God doesn't demand your holiness, faithfulness, or obedience in order to be saved. Receiving Jesus as your savior is all that's required for salvation, which means you already have eternal life with Him. If basic salvation and security in heaven is all you want, then your faith that Jesus Christ is your Savior and the only God of this world means you have it!

Sin does not affect how much God loves you and what He offers to you. God will still love you and even take care of you when you're in sinful patterns in your life. If you come from a religious background then this may be a difficult thing for you to understand, but it's true. So technically that means you shouldn't have to change, right?

Your salvation may be secured by faith, but truly understanding God's gift of salvation means receiving all that has been made available to you. God has a greater plan for you. He wants more from you. If you would like to inherit the kingdom of heaven and see Jesus restore every ounce of the life that He intended for you before He even created the world, then read on. If you would like to receive all He did, then let's talk about grace.

There was a time when there were stricter rules to keep us in our place, but we are now governed through relationship because of Jesus. Living in this age of a New Covenant with God means that we have been given grace unlike those who lived in the times of the Old Covenant. Today we have the Holy Spirit living and dwelling inside us, which couldn't even be said about Adam and Eve in their paradise. They walked with God in Eden, and now He lives in us and works through us. The fact that we never have to live even one moment of our life without His presence in our hearts is a gift of immeasurable worth.

Sexual sin, however, keeps us from fully benefiting from our relationship with God. It interrupts God's plan to return us to Eden, where we can eat of the Tree of Life (Jesus) and live long, healthy lives in His presence. My relationship with God shapes my heart, and in return, I walk in freedom from sin. If we won't partner with God in this New Covenant and allow the Holy Spirit to guide us, then we'll see this gift of grace as license or permission to break the rules; our liberty will degrade into sin.

We've seen this a lot through the ages. The Corinthians in the New Testament heard the full gospel, but they used selective hearing. The end result was a community that worked to take advantage of their grace and work around the Word of God to their own selfish ends. These people, like many of us, didn't understand the Lordship of the gospel. When you don't understand His Lordship, you will take this grace message and turn it into a self-serving religion.

What shall we say then? Are we to continue in sin that grace may abound? By no means! How can we who died to sin still live in it? Do you not know that all of us who have been baptized into Christ Jesus were baptized into his death? We were buried therefore with him by baptism into death, in order that, just as Christ was raised from the dead by the glory of the Father, we too might walk in newness of life. (Romans 6:1-4 ESV)

Here Paul addresses those who are still bound to sinful patterns, those who believe that they're hopeless sinners at their core, those who believe they've been given permission to sin. **This identity is one of an addict.** For these people, the gospel of good news is impotent. Their lives are defined by the act of receiving this gift of salvation and then remaining unresponsive to all it provides. Paul also explains very clearly to us in Romans that we are dead to sin and that we have a new nature.

He goes on to tell us that we are partnering with Satan when we willfully walk in sin, and Satan is the author of destruction. The result of believing that you're an addict is that you'll always see your nature (who you are and how you act) as one that can't break free from sin. This is a lie. Sin may change and distort how you see God, but it doesn't change the way God sees you. You are not a *sinner* or an *addict* because God does not define you as such. He defines you as a *daughter*.

Boundaries vs. Rules

Do you want God to be your master or your friend? How you see God will greatly influence the posture you take when you go to Him and how you react to His guidance. My relationship with Him matured when I began to mature, and after submitting to Him I gave up that self-defeating, Old Testament focus on *rules* and moved into a relationship of trust and listening to His voice. The longer I remained in that relationship, the more I broke free from sin and began to see Him clearly, even during times when I didn't understand what He was doing or why.

When I first returned to God He was loving, yet firm. That was what I needed at the time. This period of immaturity was a period where I strongly felt His guidance. I can remember many times when the Lord gave me very clear instructions regarding what I was to do and to whom I was to speak. He was stern in His efforts to remove me from the unhealthy world I had created around me.

If a young child is running toward the street, you yell firmly for them to stop. You do the same if they're about to touch a hot stove. It's easy for the child in either of these cases to see you as a mean old grownup who just likes to yell at them and keep them from having fun. Similarly, when we sin and step outside the boundaries God has set for us, it's easy to see Him as an aggressive figure. If we live a self-serving life and always need discipline, we'll only know Him as a parent who urgently pulls us away from what we're running toward.

But as it is with a parent and a young child, God and I grew out of that stage. My obedience helped build trust and intimacy over time. Instead of looking for loopholes and running toward sin and feebly trying to prop up my failings, now I find myself in a relationship of conversations and invitations.

Jesus' words in the Gospel of John are alive and working in my life:

> *These things I have spoken to you, that my joy may be in you, and that your joy may be full. This is my commandment, that you love one another as I have loved you. Greater love has no one than this, that someone lay down his life for his friends. You are my friends if you do what I command you. No longer do I call you servants, for the servant does not know what his master is doing; but I have called you friends, for all that I have heard from my Father I have made known to you. You did not choose me, but I chose you and appointed you that you should go and bear fruit and that your fruit should abide, so that whatever you ask the Father in my name, he may give it to you.* (John 15:11-16 ESV)

The longer I live in liberty and freedom, the more fulfilling my friendship with God becomes. I still face pain, heartache, and many challenges. Sometimes it takes a lot of effort to walk out relationships and callings, and our earthly bodies are naturally subject to flaws and decay. Everything worth having requires work. However, I can't properly express my gratitude that I'm no longer in a place of delusion, self-destruction, and self-service, believing the lie that the things seeking to bind me actually brought me power. I'm so glad I learned that independence does not equal power; giving my power over to Him gives me the *true* power I was looking for all along.

I most certainly could have continued in my sinful ways, digging myself deeper and deeper into my pit of misery, and He still would have loved me. God is always pursuing you with open arms, but He can't force you to take His hand. Scripture tells us that God does reach a point where He will hand you over to the things that you're chasing after. I believe He did this in my most destructive years, because I experienced no peace or joy during that time. It was when I finally asked for help that I found Him right next to me.

The longer you live in grace the more you realize that your actions affect God, and you start to lean on Him when He asks you to make adjustments. This is the faith that pleases Him. This is done not out of terror, but out of love. There's a holy fear that develops inside you when you pursue a deeper relationship with the Lord, but instead of a fear of being punished, it's a fear more akin to awe and wonder at His power and depths.

If I ever chose to suddenly turn around and knock over all the boundaries He's rebuilt around me, it would be easy to slip back into my old habits. More than just rebuilding my boundaries, however, He has also fortified my heart. Those temptations have dissipated because behavior that's birthed out of a loving relationship is solid, and the trust we've built with each other can't be knocked down easily.

Therefore, I am not an addict, and in no way do I ever identify as an addict. I confess the sin and admit my need for His grace in order to change my thinking, but the sin is not my identity. To think otherwise would be to undermine the work of the Cross.

Now you are no longer a slave but God's own child. And since you are his child, God has made you his heir. (Galatians 4:7 NLT)

How can you be a new creation in Christ and still have deep longings and desires for the things that are called sinful? How can you have a new nature and still remain bound to patterns that you can't break free from? The answer is, you can't. You can be free today. Your mind can be renewed as you walk away from sin and receive the truth that God loves you.

Breaking Free from Pornography

I can think of countless times I stood in front of my pornography problem and threw sticks at it, trying to shoo it away. I tried to reason with myself. "I'll try harder next time," I would say, "I just need to concentrate more." Yet, I would inevitably fall back into the same patterns and wind up back at the starting point. Like a prisoner determined to pull my arms free from my chains, the harder I tried, the more bruised and bloody I became. I denied the truth:

I had bowed to another.

I had become imprisoned.

I was not free.

The last time I watched pornography I was in one of the most epic "dark night of the soul" periods of my life. Imagine losing nearly everything that you consider precious and safe, then heap a massive helping of guilt on top of that. And after that final viewing, I decided I couldn't continue this power struggle any longer, I couldn't handle being defeated again and again. It felt like I was pulling my arms out of their sockets to forcibly pull myself free from my chains. It was then that I truly came to understand that only God was able to free me from this pattern of sin. I realized that if I was going to believe that Jesus existed, died on a cross, rose again, and speaks to me personally on a daily basis, I *had* to believe His promise that I could be free. I had to come to the end of myself. My attempts to self-regulate and shoo my problem away had to end as well.

There were times during this period of my life when I experienced His presence in a powerful way in a public church setting, with other people there to witness my encounter, but those moments were never my greatest breakthroughs. It's fun and flashy to see this kind of experience as the *Big Encounter* that changes everything—and hey, maybe that's how it will work for you—but personally, my greatest moments of freedom were in the quiet of my room.

When He and I were alone, and I struggled to understand my heart and what it needed. When I sat with Him in the loneliness and defeat of my life, wanting so desperately to return to the things that once comforted me but keeping my focus on Him instead. When I ripped myself away from the hateful god of this world that commanded me to cower in fear and isolation and fell into the arms of the God that calmly offered His love. In these quiet moments of vulnerability, He asked me to trust Him.

This act of humility and new understanding of His love gave me the power to stop self-pacifying through pornography. My new ability didn't come from my own will alone. The more I became aware of His presence, and the closer I came to the end of myself, the more I realized that His pursuit of me had been continual all along. His feelings for me had never changed and would *never* change.

God is Safe

In *The Lion, the Witch, and the Wardrobe*, Lucky and Susan ask if Aslan the great lion (symbolic of Jesus) is safe. Mr. Beaver replies, "Who said anything about safe? 'Course he isn't safe. But he's good. He's the King, I tell you."

I believe the idea that God is unsafe and capable of harming us is a falsehood. I reject the notion that God is an angry beast, ready to devour me the second I step out of line. It's unbiblical and incorrect, and this can lead us to believe our hearts aren't safe with God and keep many people bound in sin.

"God is love." (1 John 4:8 NLT)

Merriam Webster's definition of *safe* is, "secure from threat of danger, harm, or loss." I will say that serving a loving God can often involve risk. Awful things can happen in our lives, even when we know God. We all experience pain, absolutely. But God is safe. You can trust Him with all that you are, and He cares about the things you care about. He is a good father. Any other god that you've attached yourself to is *not* safe and that attachment can definitely harm you. When this happens, and you find yourself hurt, it's not because God is punishing you; it's because breaking your attachments to things of this world can be painful and messy.

As of now, I've been free from the pornography cycle for eleven years, and honestly, I have no temptation to return to it. Porn has lost its appeal for me—lost its hook in my life. When I viewed pornography for the last time, I believe the Lord gifted me with a revelation in order to solidify my freedom. And the interesting thing is that this revelation didn't come at the end of many years of constant usage; it came after I had already begun to walk out my freedom. In fact, I had been through many periods in my walk with the Lord where I would go without pornography for months. As I walked with Him more closely, my old patterns gave way to healthy ones and porn became less and less of a temptation.

Leading up to my final viewing, I had been walking free from pornography for a long time. After being married for a year, however, I discovered some very upsetting things about my husband. We worked through them and now have a restored marriage (that's a subject for another book), but at the time I found myself in the deepest pit of despair I could imagine. This was that "dark night of the soul" I was talking about. My heart was broken clean in two, and I fell back on my old lover, pornography.

When I was done watching, feeling helpless and alone with my pain, the Lord met me. In this moment He didn't say anything, yet He did open my eyes to the future. I saw a clear revelation that my marriage would stay in brokenness if I returned to pornography now. The knowledge that He had so much compassion for me when I ran to Him for comfort and strength was what had kept me free from porn up to that point, and I knew that if I chose to let go of His hand now, it would destroy my marriage and prevent the Lord from restoring it.

I also caught a glimpse of our future children being bound by the same brokenness because they were raised in a home where sin was allowed to steal the joys and purity of sex. Even though I was so angry with my husband and felt utterly betrayed by him, I could see that walking away from the new place of grace the Lord had brought me to would harm not only our lives, but the lives of our children as well.

I also saw what would happen to *me* if I opened this door again.

For no other foundation can anyone lay than that which is laid, which is Jesus Christ. Now if anyone builds on this foundation with gold, silver, precious stones, wood, hay, straw, each one's work will become clear; for the Day will declare it, because it will be revealed by fire; and the fire will test each one's work, of what sort it is. If anyone's work which he has built on it endures, he will receive a reward. If anyone's work is burned, he will suffer loss; but he himself will be saved, yet so as through fire. Do you not know that you are the temple of God and that the Spirit of God dwells in you? If anyone defiles the temple of God, God will destroy him. For the temple of God is holy, which temple you are. (1 Corinthians 3:11-17 NKJV)

I saw myself standing before God at the end of my life, giving an account of what had happened to my marriage and my family. I saw myself describing a life that was unable to give Him the glory He so wonderfully deserves. This vision wasn't meant to be harsh or critical. It wasn't His way of scolding me, or rubbing my face in what I'd done, or gearing up to punish me. All justice was fulfilled by Jesus, who took our sin upon Himself. No, this was simply a moment of sober clarity.

He was the one who defined me, loved me unconditionally, and fought for my heart, and I could finally see that walking out my trauma through my own means would be to rob Him of my love.

If the enemy was successful in entrapping my life, I would reach the end with nothing to show for it. When everything burned away in that moment, there would be nothing left of my actions to be jewels in my crown to toss at the Lord's feet (See Rev. 4:10). With this immense love that He had for me, how could I possibly waste my precious life? How could I go down this path when He had relentlessly shown me that this was worth everything to Him?

So that was that. I yielded to God, asked Him to forgive me, and committed to ending my pornography habit. I had gained a new perspective on the worth of my life and the costliness of my sexual sin. Pornography, as a means of coping with life, was simply done.

Relationship

Understanding the value of relationship is key to understanding sexual brokenness, because *sexual brokenness is a relational issue,* and that includes both relationship with God and others. Pornography is not the root cause of your sin; it's a symptom of it. That's why you will not see freedom if you try to fight this alone; you need relationship with the Holy Spirit and other believers to help you get to the root of the issue. The enemy knows that no outside source can penetrate this blanket of lies he's thrown over you if he can convince you to keep everything in the dark while you continue to try to fix it yourself. If you have a deadly infection, you can take all the Tylenol you want to get that fever down, but you're not going to get better until that infection is gone.

The Word promises us that Jesus will finish what He starts in your life (see Heb. 12:2). He has a detailed road map for bringing you to freedom, and if you allow Him to guide you, that road map will lead you to several people who can aid in your restoration process. Just remember that each of these people will play their own part; no individual person makes up the whole map. Sometimes the part a person plays is a big one, and sometimes it's relatively small. It's important not to become offended or start to withdraw if you find that certain people fail to meet your expectations, especially considering your expectations might be skewed.

You need Jesus and other people in order to cultivate freedom, but you are solely responsible for moving forward in this journey. No one can do that part for you. The more humility and responsibility you exhibit in your life, the easier this will all be. You might make mistakes. The people He brings into your life might make mistakes. However, that's the beauty of vulnerability and learning to trust in relationships; it can be messy and beautiful all at the same time. You are brave, and He will guide you! Stay with it!

Reaching Out

After receiving forgiveness and establishing God's guidance in your life, the first and most vital step toward freedom is reaching out and asking for help. The end result of finding someone to help walk you through this process isn't all you're after here; even just the act of reaching out is beneficial. First, it takes a tremendous amount of bravery and a great conscious effort to bring this issue to another person, so this is a great breakthrough all on its own. It represents how completely you have refocused on the image of the woman you were created to be. Then, if these issues have caused you to become guarded and isolated, this simple act helps reestablish your place in the church community. To go to your community for help is to be a part of that community. And even if your community isn't yet comfortable talking about masturbation and pornography, you become part of the solution and help shift the culture by openly asking for help. You lead by example through your vulnerability.

Reaching out and confessing what you've previously hidden is a biblical mandate we see clearly in scripture. James urges us:

Confess your trespasses to one another, and pray for one another, that you may be healed. The effective, fervent prayer of a righteous man avails much. (James 5:16 NKJV)

Confessing our sin accomplishes these three things:

1. It brings the sin into the light so that you can begin to deal with it. Hiding your sin brings death, therefore bringing it out into the open is an act of life.

2. It brings the sin to the attention of leadership, letting them know that there's something within their congregation that needs addressing. If everyone does this, the leadership will be able to better identify the issue and provide help and education to its congregation.

3. It allows for a deepening of relationships within a healthy church community. Opening up to another person about your sin is a very special and beautiful thing and cultivating that kind of culture breathes life into the congregation.

It's very possible that you've already tried doing this and have faced refusal or even rejection. I'm very sorry if you have made yourself vulnerable and been turned away. Not everyone is mature in their faith. My advice is to get up, dust yourself off, and try again with someone else. I commend you for your courage if you feel that you have exhausted the resources at your church, reached out to multiple trusted leaders, and still haven't found anyone willing to help you. To face one rejection is hard enough, but to face many takes a lot of strength.

At this point, I would suggest looking into other local churches and even Online resources. Things may take time, and the church is still working through our puritan attitude regarding sex. What is unfamiliar and uncomfortable for one generation can become commonplace for the next. You just have to keep looking for mature believers who are strong and steady in their faith that you can go to for help. These churches and people are all laid out on Jesus' road map; you just have to keep your foot on the gas.

Naturally, this is all easier said than done. You're not going to feel like doing this, and sometimes it may feel like an impossibly unpleasant task. However, soon you'll begin to discover the beauty in doing what's uncomfortable in order to gain a great reward. I promise you, what is difficult now will not be difficult later. The more transparent you become, the more comfortable you will be with your transparency.

I mean hey, look at me! If you went back in time to when I was in ministry school and told me that this book would one day exist, I think I would probably curl up into a mortified little ball and just die. Or maybe I would become a super villain bent on destroying every last pencil, pen, shred of paper, and computer in existence so that writing this book would be impossible. Yet, here we are, and although I can certainly appreciate the magnitude of writing an entire book about what were once, essentially, my dirty little secrets, I feel no fear or doubt about it whatsoever. In fact, the idea that my vulnerability may educate and inspire someone makes me eager to do so! I've overcome so much, and Jesus receives all the credit for those victories in my life!

The enemy's job is to build up walls around your life and convince you that isolation equals safety. By keeping your sin secret, you have reinforced those walls. Some people have even written off this isolation as merely being a part of their personality, saying things like, "Well, I'm a very private person. I could never do that…" This is one of the cleverest lies the enemy has in this situation. If something prevents you from opening up to others and bringing your sin into the light and deepening your relationships as a result, it is not a part of your identity. It wouldn't be vulnerability if it didn't require discomfort and risk, and this is true for even the most brazen, extroverted person on the planet. Always try to identify when your beliefs about your personality may be keeping you bound.

When talking about opening up to other believers, it's important to establish what that means. I'm definitely not suggesting that you air your dirty laundry in front of everyone you come across. It's all about finding safe and mature people who have overcome their own struggles and who demonstrate strength and trustworthiness. Ideally, this means other women, preferably those in pastoral leadership. If you go to a larger church, then you can look to the leaders of your community groups. Barring that, even another member of your church can be a great resource, especially if that person has faced the same problems you face or if they act as an elder in your life.

If you don't currently attend a church, well...then that's going to be your first step. Being in a church community is absolutely necessary in overcoming sexual brokenness. Accountability is the ongoing effort to connect with people who can provide you with insight.

Now this may sound a little strange but loving yourself is not the first step toward freedom. I know this probably goes against every self-help book and motivational speaker on the planet, but the idea of loving yourself first just isn't biblical. One main reason you're having these issues is that your perception of yourself is skewed. You need to focus on how much God loves you—pray, meditate on it, ask Him about it—and as you do this, things will become clearer and clearer. Your ability to better love yourself and others will come through this. He teaches us how to love because He is love.

In this the love of God was manifested toward us, that God has sent His only begotten Son into the world, that we might live through Him. In this is love, not that we loved God, but that He loved us and sent His Son to be the propitiation for our sins.

Beloved, if God so loved us, we also ought to love one another.
(1 John 4:9-11 NKJV)

Your Sex Life Will Be Different

Sex and sensitivity are going to be different when you've stopped partnering with lust. It's not going to be about instant gratification anymore. Your sex drive will take time to adjust and become sensitive again. Your hormones and even vagina will take time to adjust to the new signals being sent out from your brain.

For married women walking away from pornography, your ability to experience sexual arousal is not going to be at the same level it once was. Don't be discouraged if you have to relearn how to orgasm with your husband. The Lord will teach you how to focus on loving your husband, and my prayer is that you're married to someone who carries His heart, just as you do. You are called to this, to restore your marriage and make it strong according to God's own vision. Stay in it. Never lose hope while He rebuilds your ability to become intimate.

For single women who break free of lust, remember that this isn't just for your benefit but for your future family's benefit as well. Your new clarity and motivation will help you navigate singleness in a healthy way as He restores your sex drive. For you, this is about receiving the grace for your drive to be calmed and quieted. Again, as you break free from self-centeredness and the urge to self-comfort, there will be a struggle. However, remind yourself why you choose to follow the Lord and always keep that vision in front of you.

Remind yourself that being bound by pornography will hinder your ability to relate to any man you date, and that breaking God's boundaries will likely attract a man who does the same. Remind yourself that you are not a helpless woman who needs to be rescued and that a man won't bring your chaos to order. You are a powerful woman in a partnership with God.

Whether you're married or single, your desires can and will change when you stay on track and leave behind your old patterns of selfishness. Become a student of God's love, and He will walk you through it.

Practical Steps for Single Women

For those of you who are single and living alone, I can't recommend getting a Spirit-filled roommate highly enough. First, and most obviously, having another person in the house just makes it harder to watch porn and masturbate. When you live alone, your home is a place where you can retreat and act on your urges whenever you want, but having someone else in that space creates a very different dynamic. More deeply, though, having a roommate that shares some of your interests can help bring you out of isolation and help you start building healthier patterns.

Even more so than regular friends, roommates can satisfy some of your needs for relationship. God doesn't intend for any of us to live in solitude, struggling and suffering on our own. He built us to crave friendships and thrive when we're around others that support us. Even completely separate from sexual issues, our brains need a certain level of stimulation, and it's all too easy to slip into the comfort of routine and become depressed when living alone. A roommate can bring new life into your home, share in your joys and struggles, and provide a healthy way to process at the end of the day.

So, get a roommate, or even a few. Have fun and be goofy with them. Go on adventures with them. Do new things and try new foods together. Learn to exercise your passion for life with them. If you're on a road trip to the Grand Canyon, then you're too busy for porn. And while roomies are definitely ideal, this applies to regular friendships as well. Whatever the case, and whoever you may find, it's important to sow into the friendships around you while you address the issues surrounding your pornography usage.

As you grow in relationships with God and others, it's also important to start holding yourself accountable as you manage your sex drive. Like I said before, tracking your cycle will give you insight into what times of the month you may be the horniest. Knowing that you're about to ovulate and planning accordingly empowers you to avoid moments of weakness.

You may want to stay away from romantic movies or books (even if they are "clean"). Working out is a really great way to alleviate some of the sexual tension you may be experiencing. Also be aware of who you hang out with and how you interact with them during these times. Growing male friendships is part of God's plan for your social development, but if you're currently in a more vulnerable point of your cycle, or you're just randomly feeling randy, keep an eye on things and avoid potentially uncomfortable situations. Honor the sex drive in all its wild beauty.

Just remember that being *aware* does not equal being *afraid*. This is about being in tune with your body, not denying yourself life experiences because you're scared of failure. Identify the triggers that lead you to viewing porn and use that knowledge to set up healthy boundaries. Track what happens in your body in order to better connect yourself with God and your friends and family. This way, when the sexual tension is at its peak, you can thank God that he gave you a very healthy sex drive instead of cursing your hormones.

Lastly, I should mention that there may be some of you who have been bound by pornography for so long that you've found it hard to make and keep friends. It may have pulled you away from many great experiences and caused you to retreat from people because of feelings of rejection and shame. I can certainly relate to this, as during the peaks of my own usage I isolated myself. Now that you're staying accountable and becoming more aware of your body, getting out and connecting with people will come more easily. Friendship isn't always a speedy process, but God has placed the right people around you if you're willing to go out and look.

Practical Steps for Married Women

The first step is to have a conversation with your husband, as painful or embarrassing as the idea may be. If he's a believer, then hopefully your marriage has a foundation of commitment, trust, and forgiveness. If he becomes angry and tries to shame you, point out that you are hurting and attempting to heal your marriage by bringing this problem to him.

And really, it might be easier to broach the subject than you think, because there's a good chance he already suspects something is going on. Considering the pervasiveness of the problem, he may even be hiding pornography usage himself. If so, then your act of honesty might even help him with his own freedom. A true spirit-filled man of God will see the pain this is causing you and want to seek freedom for both himself and the wife he loves.

If you find that he's using pornography and tries to downplay or dismiss the problem, or even supports the idea of using porn as a sexual aid, don't buy into it. He's afraid of losing his vice, so he's attempting to normalize it. This is a problem you need to bring to God *together*. Married women often turn to pornography because of an inability to connect with their spouses emotionally and sexually. If this is the case for you, then a marriage counselor would be a good resource as you go about restoring your marriage. Licensed counselors are fine, but also look into your church community for leadership that may offer such services.

Pornography can sometimes open the door to other adulterous actions such as Online video chats or flirting with acquaintances. In this case, an immediate severing of all sexual relationships you've engaged in (whether emotional or physical) is vital. If you want to restore your marriage then bringing this to the light is completely necessary, no matter how difficult it may be.

Be willing to put everything on the table. Remember that when we submit to God's will, He can perform miracles. You may not feel like you love your spouse anymore, but these emotions can be restored as you rebuild intimacy through repentance and forgiveness. You have meditated on damaging images and engaged in damaging relationships, and Timothy 4 tells us that participating in prolonged sin sears our conscious and creates a calloused heart. It will take time to renew your mind and heart. It will take time to rebuild trust and reignite the hearts of both you and your husband.

Prayer of Repentance

Women often ask me if they'll always struggle with pornography and/or masturbation. I tell them that God is able to break the bondage of sin, but they'll always have a vagina. The things that tempt us will always exist, no matter who we are. That's what it is to be human. When we bring our weaknesses to the Lord, however, they become strengths. Temptations lose their hold. And as long as we continue leaning on Him and cultivating healthy thoughts and habits, life doesn't have to be an all-consuming struggle. Just remember that **everlasting freedom is a moment-by-moment commitment.**

Maybe you've begun the process of freeing yourself from pornography before, or maybe this is the first time you've allowed God into this broken area. Either way, do not lose hope. God promises to complete what he started in you, and you will become free from pornography if you're willing to stay connected to Him. Sometimes our own fear and pride can slow us down or veer us from the road He's laid out for us. If you feel this is the case for you, please take a moment to pray this prayer:

Jesus, I give you full access to my heart, mind, and actions. I desire to know you in the depths of this pain. Please forgive me for attempting to do things my way. I am sorry for how I have dishonored myself. I am sorry for hurting others. I see now that I have deviated from the path you set for me, and that this grieves you. Please teach me about your love and your desire to see me free. Reveal lies that I have believed concerning pornography and my ability to stay free from it. Break every chain that binds me from freedom and give me the tenacity to continue on this path. Thank you for your forgiveness and love. Amen!

Chapter Seven

Same-Sex Attraction

"Everyone struggles with their sexuality to some degree, and a loving, grace-filled church community is the place that can help us to heal."

—Sy Rogers

So far, we've talked about God's original vision for sex and for the good plan that He has for our sexual intimacy. However, in this chapter we're going to head in a slightly different direction and cover the topic of same-sex attraction and homosexuality. Even if this doesn't exactly pertain to you, I urge you to read on anyway.

There has been a dramatic culture shift in recent years, and homosexuality is now prevalent and even encouraged in our society. We need a loving and understanding Christian response to this shift, and to know the mind of the Lord, so that we don't fall into the two most common traps surrounding homosexuality: we don't want to be unloving and condemn anyone, but we also don't want to embrace bondage and simply dismiss it as a different form of love.

Every one of us needs the wisdom of the Lord in order to rightly discern how to deal with these issues.

A Changing Landscape

Our culture's definition of sexuality is constantly shifting and changing. Vocabulary and terminology surrounding homosexuality is one of the most emotionally charged subjects of our day. This is a result of the diversification of the LGBTQ community (Lesbian, Gay, Bisexual, Transgender, Queer/ Questioning) as it has sought its own identity and voice. Christian churches—especially those in America—face a growing tension between the desire to create an atmosphere where the LGBTQ community is heard and valued and the desire to express biblical truths that Christian doctrine has stood on since the resurrection of Jesus.

I've found that the healthiest and most impactful churches are the ones that attempt to bridge the gap between the LGBTQ community and the heart of evangelism by inviting hard conversations and seeking reconciliation for the historic lack of respect and care seen in our churches for those in this community. And while a heart of evangelism is necessary to reach those who do not know Christ, it's important to utilize different modes of discussion when people from the LGBTQ community desire to get to know Jesus and join church communities. How I speak to a non-believer on this issue will be different from how I speak to a believer, because they each have different knowledge of God. Clear and adaptive communication is important when reaching outside of a familiar circle.

Believers who are effective at ministering to the LGBTQ community remain within that state of tension by never falling on the side of either rejection or acceptance. It's all about building relationships while keeping your vision fixed on the truth of the gospel; the goal is always to connect others to Jesus in order to bring them to the kingdom of God. Salvation may be the first step, but believing that Jesus is your Savior and walking in your Christian identity are two very different things. It's up to those who have walked in the transformative power of the Holy Spirit to help others find what's available for them. It's great when a believer steps into their inheritance, but how will anyone else know how to step into theirs if we don't tell them?

In the following chapters I'll define some terminology and speak from my own experiences with homosexuality. Please keep in mind that none of the wording I use is meant to disrespect or limit anyone. Like I said, the landscape is always changing and the list of words and phrases that are deemed appropriate to use changes with it. The following is simply my way of communicating what I believe to be God's desire to see restoration in the lives of men and women who face same-sex attraction. It's by no means exhaustive, but hopefully it will bring some clarity to the conversation.

The Error of Defining Sexual Identity Outside of God's Word

When discussing secular beliefs about sexuality, it's important to discuss one of our society's greatest influencers when it comes to personhood, Sigmund Freud. Freud was a neurologist and the founder of psychoanalysis, whose work was dedicated to studying human behavior. Though his work was—and still is—highly controversial, Freud contributed hugely to what is now considered the foundation of psychologically understanding human sexuality.

His theory was that humans are comprised of three parts: the Id, Ego, and Superego. This is something of a trilogy of personhood, and the idea is that these parts are in a constant wrestling match. The Id represents the primal urges of a human, the Superego represents the collective social conscious that's influenced by external sources such as parents, religion, society, etc., and the Ego is the worn-out middle man who represents your own thoughts and feelings and is trying to make sense of it all.

Freud believed that conflict arises when the Id is trying to express its primal needs, but the Superego is hindered by the pressures of social influence. He also believed that it's necessary to get in touch with the Id and even side with it sometimes by casting off the societal restraints affecting the Superego. If you grew up with a strict religious background and had a desire to party, Freud would tell you to get out there and party until you dropped. His thinking was that this was the way to resolve the conflict between a person's attractions and the learned structure of society.

Humans are prone to several of these "primal urges" (aggression, for example), but sex was at the forefront of Freud's research and theories. He believed all humans have unconscious sexual impulses that are constantly struggling for freedom from those societal influences that hold them back. He reduced human sexuality to a very animalistic thing, which is contrary to the self-controlled and dignified image of sex we see in the Bible.

Freud was an atheist and believed that God is an illusion invented by our minds because of our own impulsive needs. Even though he was in great error with his work, I do believe he was right in recognizing the relationship between the body and what you could define as the spirit. He attempted to resolve the conflict that arises when the body fights the forces that want to control it. The problem was that he falsely believed that all boundaries are restraining and create conflict, when the Bible tells us that the opposite is true. Since Freud pushed God out of the picture, he came to the conclusion that a person's sexual desires represented their true identity. As believers, however, we know that our desires are a part of us, but they do not define us and can change as we develop a relationship with Jesus.

Discover Eden

Freud Preaching from the Back Pew

Just as Freud's worldview affected society's beliefs regarding sex, it's also creeped into our church culture when it comes to explaining our sexual desires. It's important to realize when we're adopting these views and identify them as ungodly.

First, some women believe that their same-sex attraction is evidence that God created them to be gay, bisexual, transgender, etc. This is that Freudian idea that your core identity is tied to whatever you're aroused by or drawn to. There is, of course, no denying that there are women who are attracted to the same sex. What's important for every Jesus-loving woman to understand is that even though we are all born into a fallen and sinful world, we do not have to live in that world's sinful patterns.

Second, for a moment let's picture a woman who has struggled with same-sex attraction but is in the process of working with the Lord to change. Some other believers might watch the rate at which she's changing her attractions a little too closely or observe that even after a good amount of time she still struggles with her attractions. These believers might begin to reason that there must be an indwelling sin within her that some people call a "sin nature." This is the very Freudian idea that no matter what we do or how close we get to God, our sin nature will always be alive and kicking and waiting for the right moment to burst out, like a little monster that lives inside us.

This idea is entirely false. If you are a believer in Christ, there is no inner sin nature that draws you to the idea of sleeping with women. There is no sin nature that will torment you for the rest of your life, constantly threatening to take over and cause you to lose control. You don't have to walk around forever with a sign pinned to your back that reads, "If I lose consciousness and become a giant, hairy, girl-chasing monster, please restrain me and return me to the following address when I turn back into my Christian girl form." The idea that there is a sexually deviant animal living in your basement, and that you have to beat it down daily with scripture memorization and makeup tutorials, is absurd. Your nature is new in Christ. Freud's Id monster does not exist, because it died along with Christ.

This doesn't mean that you won't struggle in your walk to achieve this new identity. There's no instant fix—only a process. Your sexual desires will change as you learn to follow the Lord, and you'll come to understand that every day you can partner with a godly plan or a demonic one. Just remember that being a slave to emotions and appetites that have been cultivated outside of God's will is not your identity; being the Lord's daughter is now your identity. The longer you believe in this identity and walk in these truths, the more your desires will change or subside. Instead of constantly trying to break in, soon they'll sit at the gate and try to coax you into the badlands. At that point, you'll tell them that you'd prefer to stay happy and healthy within the Lord's abundant boundaries.

You'll be safe from the fear that there is something inherently wrong and horrible about you for facing same-sex attraction. This is crucial as we look at same-sex attraction and homosexuality because our personhood is defined as a "new creation" by our faith in Jesus.

Therefore, if anyone is in Christ, he is a new creation; old things have passed away; behold, all things have become new. (2 Corinthians 5:17 NKJV)

We don't deny that we are born into a world that is corrupt and experiencing the effects of sin. We do, however, know that while sin can affect our original natures and lead us to unhealthy desires outside of God's boundaries, those natures are now affected even more greatly by our walk with Christ. Our society is rapidly adopting the idea that we're born with innate sexual desires that are fixed and cannot change, but this is contrary to what scripture teaches, and takes away all personal responsibility and accountability from an individual for their sexual behavior.

Homosexuality

Homosexuality is characterized by a tendency to direct sexual desire toward or engage in sexual activity with persons of the same sex. **Same-sex attraction (SSA)** is a term often used to describe having these kinds of desires, though it doesn't necessarily mean those desires are being acted upon. Further, there are people who are attracted to the same sex, and who even engage in sexual activities with them, yet do not define themselves as homosexual. As I said, in the LGBTQ community the landscape is ever-changing as social norms, political rallying, and religious institutions all attempt to place definitions on sexuality and what it can be.

Homosexual orientation is another term that is often brought up when describing those experiencing same-sex attraction, although it's becoming hard to distinguish if users of the term (even in the Christian community) believe that God can shift desires and attractions, or if they believe it's all fixed. What's important is to understand what scripture says about homosexuality and what the gospel offers for those who experience same-sex attraction.

Same-Sex Attraction

There's a heated debate going on regarding the origins of homosexuality. There are some that believe homosexuality is fixed and set by nature; in other words, you're born that way. Others believe that it's a result of nurture; your sexual attractions are fluid and can be altered by your environmental circumstances. Those in the nature camp believe it's inhuman to question or deny any form of sexuality. The nurture camp believes that, much like other appetites that are affected by brain chemistry and hormones, this is a part of a person that can change.

As of today, there is no solid scientific evidence of a homosexual gene, and many people believe that if one is found, it will put an end to the debate for good. However, even if they do find causal genetic markers, there's no denying that environment still plays a factor in influencing these markers. It would only point more clearly to the fact that we are born into a fallen world in need of restoration.

There are genetic factors that cause physical defects, deficiencies, obesity (the struggle is real), depression, acid reflux—the list goes on and on. Many problems can be caused by outside forces as well as biological factors, but it's a scientific fact that genes can play a large part in all this. Despite these issues being genetic—despite people being "born that way"—we choose to address and solve these issues.

Even if sexual desires are found to be genetically influenced, scripture still tells us that they belong within God's boundaries. We *all* suffer the effects of sin in our bodies and our minds, in many different ways. We *all* need a savior, whether we're fat or have bad breath or are attracted to the same sex. The good news is that whatever the issue, it will be transformed by the renewing of our mind in Christ.

Despite what the media and the greater gay community would have you believe, there are gay non-Christians who actually *don't* want to experience same-sex attraction for reasons other than religious ones. It's true that many people accept and pursue these feelings, but many others just don't want them. This happens because same-sex attraction is not frequently a conscious choice. I've met many Christians who believe gay people are gay because they just love being deviant and making God angry, or some nonsense like that. But it's not so black and white as that. The truth is that nature and nurture are not mutually exclusive. In other words, your spirit becomes a new creation when you're a believer, but your soul and body still need to be renewed. Some believers face same-sex attraction because of a broken identity that needs to be restored by the Lord.

In many cases, including my own, same-sex attraction arises early in sexual development. It can also develop over time due to various circumstances. Some people have always believed that they were gay, and others experience what the world would call an "awakening," where they finally come to accept and believe it. Sexual abuse, divorce, incarceration, parental rejection, lack of parental influence, and sexual curiosity are just a few examples of factors that can lead a person to experience same-sex attraction and even act on these desires.

Women Facing Same-Sex Attraction

Marriage is not a "remedy" in dealing with same sex attraction. A relationship status does not change your sexual wholeness. Getting married to a man does not "fix" a person who is struggling with same-sex attraction. Too often, the church community's solution is to pressure a person into marrying the first opposite-sex schmuck willing to slap a ring on them. These kinds of actions are purely surface level, much like putting a Band-Aid over a bleeding laceration, and they discount the work of the Holy Spirit in a person's life.

For all we know, the Lord may lead you to marry even when you're still experiencing some level of same-sex attraction. It's your walk, and it's always important to do what you honestly believe He's leading you to do. There's a difference, however, between walking peacefully from a place of trust and obedience and trying to force desired outcomes using our own means. If you buckle under the pressure to "fix" yourself and enter into a marriage with these issues unresolved, unhealthy results will begin to surface between you and your husband.

If you're single and you want to address same-sex attraction for the first time in your life, celibacy is an important component in your restoration. If you're involved in a same-sex relationship, fantasizing about other women, or masturbating to images of them, you will not be able to begin dealing with the underlying issues of your heart. It can feel like an impossible situation to get out of, but remember that God is infinitely helpful in calming processes that have been spinning out of control for years.

If you're married and haven't yet brought your struggle to light, yielding to the Holy Spirit is the first step. You were made for deep intimacy with your husband. The idea that you can't have a satisfying relationship with a man is a lie, and too many married Christian women have hidden their same-sex attraction because of shame. That is not God's best for you. He wants to help you get to the root of why you are struggling. Humble yourself and go to Him.

Prayer of Repentance

As someone who's addressed my own same-sex attraction and identity issues, I know for a fact that the Lord desires to set you free from the thoughts and ideas that bind you. There is a peace and a joy in my life now that I never could have imagined when I was in the depths of my shame. This peace and joy is available to you. If you would like to begin your journey with the Holy Spirit to discover your true identity, you can start with this prayer:

Jesus, I give you access to every part of me. Please forgive me for forming my identity and my opinions about myself based on my sexual attractions and desires. I receive your forgiveness today and believe that my wholeness was paid for on the Cross. You are able and willing to do so much more in my life than I can even imagine, so I open my heart to you today. Please dispel all lies about myself, you, and others that have been keeping me from my identity. I confess that my sexual attractions do not define who I am when they do not line up with your will for my life. Thank you for being a kind Father who wants His daughter to know who she was designed to be. Help me understand what it is to be a daughter who is loved unconditionally. Thank you. Amen!

Chapter Eight

Is Being Gay the Identity God Gave Me?

"When you find your definitions in God, you find the very purpose for which you were created. Put your hand into God's hand, know His absolutes, demonstrate His love, present His truth, and the message of redemption and transformation will take hold."

—Ravi Zacharias

My Story

I wasn't a pretty lesbian. Well, I think my girlfriend found me pretty, but nowadays it seems that when you turn on the TV most lesbians are gorgeous and infinitely confident. Ellen Page, Jodi Foster, Ellen DeGeneres' partner with the name that I can't pronounce…all strong, beautiful women. Nope. Not me, though. I was awkward. Precarious. Insecure. I was proud in my own shaky sort of way, but I always preferred to stay in the background.

Is Being Gay the Identity God Gave Me?

For those of you who are unfamiliar with my testimony pertaining to homosexuality, it may be helpful if I explain. Deep in the mountains of Northern California rests a little town I'll call Wilsonville. To this day, the small wooded community only houses about twelve-hundred people. My parents left their well-paying jobs in Silicon Valley and relocated there to pastor a church of about five members when I was seven years old.

Us big-city Christians contrasted sharply with the culture in this new place. As I wrote in my book, *The God of My Parents:*

If you were forced to lump all of the residents of Wilsonville into two primary groups you could call them the hippies and the rednecks. Hippies that grew pot, rednecks that cut timber, hippies that protested the cutting of timber, rednecks that smoked pot but hated the hippies, Native Americans that grew pot and cut timber, and the few that simply lived in the middle of it all.

Considering the environment in which I grew up, I think I identify more as a "missionary kid" than a "pastor's kid." I was exposed to much more non-church culture than perhaps the typical pastor's child. Outside of our tiny church was a world of vastly differing beliefs and lifestyles and, truth be told, I'm extremely thankful that I was raised in such a diverse environment. In addition to seeing the world from multiple perspectives, I learned a ton about the arts, community, the environment, and empathy to name a few things. We may have been dirt poor, but there was a richness to the community that I admire to this day.

Unfortunately, during my years in Wilsonville I experienced a lot of rejection, largely because of my weight and the fact that I always felt like an outsider because of my faith. In order to escape the pain, I made smoking pot and drinking a part of my routine.

Most of my attempts to form romantic relationships ended in heartache. I did have a few boyfriends, but nothing long-term.

I held onto the notion that I really wasn't worth pursuing, so I would pour my heart and soul into any guy that was willing to give me the time of day. This led to sexual experiences as early as middle school that continued on into high school. And as you can imagine, these sexual experiences never led to anything resembling a healthy relationship or even so much as a normal friendship with a boy. I was trading myself away for any sort of attention or validation I could get my hands on.

This process eventually wore thin and going into my senior year of high school I became callous toward guys. More and more I realized that I was always more comfortable and felt more affirmed when I was with my girlfriends. The depth of intimacy and safety I felt with my close female friends was far greater than anything I had shared with any man. And when I was honest with myself, I found that I had experienced sexual attraction to girls since pretty early on in puberty.

There was no room to discuss this in the Christian culture I grew up in, and I was confused by these feelings, so I never spoke about them. But one night, when I was drunk with some friends, I had what I believed was my grand epiphany: I was a lesbian. It seemed like the pieces of the puzzle were finally coming together for me.

I "came out" my senior year and shortly after that I left for college. Suddenly I found myself living on my own terms, finally free from all the drama and rejection of high school, and reveling in my newfound identity. For a while my life appeared to be perfect…

This new Liz certainly didn't seem perfect to my parents though. Over the years, a divide had opened between us. Mom didn't know how to handle her increasingly independent and rebellious daughter, and Dad couldn't accept my new sexual identity when he weighed it against what the Bible says about homosexuality. Despite Dad's unwavering stance and the uncomfortable gap now between us though, he always kept a hand outstretched to me. This would prove to be very important.

Fueled by my new independence and every Ani DiFranco CD ever released, I ran hard in my freedom. I enrolled in a junior college and joined the LGBTQ community at the nearby state college. I made new connections, including the romantic relationships with women that I felt I had been missing out on. And this new Age of Liz was glorious in my eyes. I had been liberated and could finally experience life to its fullest. I could finally pursue what I thought was best for me. The door had been opened and this little short-haired, pot-smoking, VW Beetle-driving chick had flown the coop. Sigmund Freud would have been proud that I had actualized my Id's strongest desires and pursued them unhindered.

Then, after only a few months, everything screeched to a halt.

Someone very close to me was diagnosed with cancer, and passed away after a very difficult struggle. After that, I spiraled like I had never spiraled before. I slipped into a heavy depression and the next year or two were a blur of self-medicating with drugs and pursuing romantic relationships. Never in all my years of confusion and rejection and aimlessness had I felt this miserable.

One afternoon I sat in my living room, blowing bong smoke into the air. Normally pot helped deaden my emotions, but now I was suddenly overwhelmed by a realization of just how deep into this pit of depression I had fallen—how disconnected I was from my family and from God. So, I began to speak to Him. I told Him I wasn't sure if I was allowed to talk to Him while I was high, but I couldn't get myself out of this pit. Suddenly the room filled with the presence of God and all at once I knew that He truly loved me.

Unfortunately, my problems did not miraculously dissipate that afternoon. For the next few days I even tried to continue my regular routine of sleep, school, pot, sleep, school, pot, and so on. Thing was, whenever I smoked I was hit with such strong panic attacks that I thought I was literally going to die. I didn't *want* to quit smoking, and the temptation didn't just instantly disappear, but I finally surrendered to the fact that God was giving me a way out.

Sober and newly committed to handing my life over to God, I reconciled with my family. I also felt led by God to enroll in a ministry school in another city. This new relationship with Him was all I cared about. I spent as much time as I could praying, worshiping, and studying the Bible. I learned a lot during this time and had experiences with God that I never thought were possible. And even during all this, I continued to experience same-sex attraction.

Wait, wait, wait, hold the phone… Seriously, Liz? Isn't this your mountaintop testimony? You submitted your life to God and still you were attracted to other women?

Yup. Aligning myself with God's will allowed me to have powerful encounters with Him where a ton of torment left my soul, but the feelings I had were still there.

These unresolved feelings started to eat away at my thought life, and I began once more to blow my world up with poor choices after finishing ministry school. (I know, quite the roller coaster ride I was on.) Thankfully though, as I mentioned earlier, I was introduced to a sexual wholeness ministry at my church with a big focus on our godly identities. It wasn't just comprised of people who experienced same-sex attraction; it covered all the areas of sexuality that aren't traditionally talked about in church settings.

We were led by a married couple who had walked through many struggles in these areas. Once a week, we came together to form a loving environment where we could not only open up and receive counsel but take in sound biblical teaching.

Is Being Gay the Identity God Gave Me?

There was no electric shock therapy, no mandatory makeup classes, no workshops on the proper way to wear a jockstrap, no deliverance room with a mop bucket where they commanded the devil out of us—none of that. The class didn't place any huge expectations on us concerning our growth in our femininity or masculinity; the only requirement was that we stay connected to the Holy Spirit and follow Christ.

We were taught how to completely depend on the work of Jesus in our daily lives and empowered to drive out the darkness by believing in His love. We were loved by people who were imperfect, who let us be our messy selves, who encouraged us to grow without measuring our progress against some man-made standard. They knew we weren't misfit castaways who needed etiquette classes, and they treated us with honor and respect as members of God's family.

Our leaders understood the foundational teachings of the gospel: repentance, forgiveness, and receiving His grace to walk out obedience. In this environment, repentance was a normal part of seeing more clearly what God had for us. And when I say "repentance" I'm not talking about us tearing our clothes and gnashing our teeth whenever we had a dirty thought. Repenting meant allowing the Holy Spirit to identify thought patterns that did not align with His truth and receiving what He had to say about these areas of our lives. When I repented, I recognized that these thoughts and emotions weren't His best for me, and I came into agreement with Him that they were not my identity.

This sounds pretty simple, but it's anything but easy; this process is costly because *transformation* is costly. It takes truly letting go. It takes meditating on the Word and spending many hours dialoguing with Him, when sometimes all you want to do is pick up the reins of your life and take control again. It takes your entire self. It's painful and beautiful.

Through the process of walking out my faith, I identified a lot of lies about myself and drove out a lot of darkness through His love and perspective. The closer I grew to God, the easier it became to spot these lies, because during my walk I learned this little tidbit: **Don't believe everything you think.** It's true that much of the darkness in my life was caused by the absence of God in my sexual expression, but much of it was also caused by my own skewed perceptions. I learned that my thought life could bring me either life or death and that basing everything on my own understanding could breed chaos and pain. This was a huge stepping stone for me.

Trust in the Lord with all your heart, and lean not on your own understanding; in all your ways acknowledge Him, and He shall direct your paths. (Proverbs 3:5-6 NKJV)

This amazing God of ours displays His infinite love by constantly reaching out and pursuing our bitter hearts no matter what we do, no matter how far we fall. But the route to healing and freedom is always through the same door, the one labeled "HUMILITY." This humility is what enables the rest of the process; it produces repentance (which is to change your mind, to see things God's way). God resists the proud. Those who decide to do life their own way without His direction and power will find it very difficult to find liberty through Him.

And He'll always let us chase after whatever we want to chase after. If we choose to worship idols, He'll hand us over to them. He gave us free will, after all. But He will continue facing us, His arms open wide, waiting for us to turn around and embrace Him. When we do, He'll gladly clear the paths that we've made a mess of.

Therefore God also gave them up to uncleanness, in the lusts of their hearts, to dishonor their bodies among themselves, who exchanged the truth of God for the lie, and worshiped and served the creature rather than the Creator, who is blessed forever. Amen. For this reason God gave them up to vile passions. For even their women exchanged the natural use for what is against nature. Likewise also the men, leaving the natural use of the woman, burned in their lust for one another, men with men committing what is shameful, and receiving in themselves the penalty of their error which was due. (Romans 1:24-27 NKJV)

When my life was a hot mess, it was pride, more than anything, that kept me from hearing and obeying God. That sounds like something of an oversimplification, but it's basic gospel. Jesus is in the business of restoring my life with whatever the enemy has stolen from it. Discipline and truth are always before me, and I always have the choice to turn to them or keep running.

Can You Be a Gay Christian?

Many well-meaning Christians have asked me if I chose to be gay, and as we've established, that was not the case. I very much had a free will growing up, but it was not a conscious effort on my part. Gay chose me. Gay had some stuff to say about me and I fell for it hook, line, and sinker. It gave me answers to questions I had in my heart about sexual attraction and belonging.

This, however, brings up another interesting question: *If being gay wasn't your choice, can you be a gay Christian?* I believe that you cannot be a gay Christian, and I would like to address two perspectives on the issue.

The first is that of both believers and non-believers who adhere to a gay theology. Gay theologians believe that God is okay with homosexual thoughts, desires, and activity. They approach the Bible with preconceived ideas and beliefs that they superimpose over scripture in order to manipulate it. They conveniently dismiss over two thousand years of doctrinal beliefs (including the entire life of

Jesus), they label the Apostles' writings as misogynistic and out of touch with today's evolved society, and often times they question the legitimacy of scripture as a whole.

There are, however, gay theologians who study the Bible and conclude that while it prohibits errant homosexual acts, God will condone a homosexual relationship as long as it's monogamous and committed. Basically, they believe that it's perfectly acceptable to identify as a gay Christian as long as you play by the rules like any believer in a faithful and committed Christian relationship.

In both the Old and New Testament, there are no positive examples of same-sex relationships. If a God-ordained, same-sex relationship existed, He would have foreseen this question long ago and given us a model to follow. He's a good father who doesn't want us to be confused about big issues like this, so they're covered by the Bible in ways we can grasp. It's a little hard for me to believe that this is one subject that just sort of slipped through the cracks for Him.

From Genesis to Revelation, the only depiction of a blessed marriage is that of a marriage between a man and a woman. Men and women contrast each other, which mirrors that beautiful balance of Christ and the Church. Attraction to the same sex is attraction to your *own image* and not a *complementary image*. If you come to scripture without bias you'll see that homosexuality is just not supported in any way, shape, or form. Growing up in the Church, I always knew this was the case. The problem was that simple belief in God didn't address what I was facing, and I had no idea what to do. I knew He didn't want me to be gay, but I was experiencing same-sex attraction, so what could I do about it?

This leads me to the next perspective I would like to discuss. There are many believers who struggle with same-sex attraction and use the term "gay Christian" to describe themselves. There is a growing number of believers who are bringing their attractions to light so that they can better express their struggles and gain a better sense of belonging. I really respect what they're doing and appreciate their desire to be understood and valued. However, I have an issue with the term "gay Christian."

The label misses the mark in multiple ways, depending on who's using it. If it's used by a Christian who has no plans to address their same-sex attractions, it's being used to communicate the idea that God approves of those attractions and that they are in line with His plan. We know that this is not the case.

But even Christians who want God to change these attractions are doing themselves and others a disservice by using the term. Calling yourself a gay Christian means you have used your sexual desires and struggles to define your entire personhood. The whole idea of allowing God to change your attractions is initiated by laying down your definition of yourself and following His definition of you.

When I was at my highest weight I did not identify as a "fat Christian," when I watch one too many episodes of Gilmore Girls in a row I'm not a "lazy Christian," and when my husband chews his food too loudly I'm not an "annoyed Christian." I'm a Christian. God tells me who I am, and I define myself by His description. This is very similar to what we talked about in chapter six when we established that it's wrong to call yourself an addict.

And not only does labeling yourself oppose God's own definition of who you are, but it acts as something of a self-fulfilling prophecy. If you call yourself a gay Christian, it's going to affect how you proceed in your walk with Him. When you slip up in your thoughts or actions, you can just chalk it up to that darned homosexuality of yours. It's just as damaging as telling yourself that you're fat, or stupid, or bad at your job. We have a way of turning our thoughts into realities, even when we don't mean to.

Finally, the term is just confusing and misleading. When most people in our secular society hear someone describe themselves as "gay," they assume that person has accepted homosexuality as their identity. If this isn't the case with you, and you no longer want to engage in homosexual behavior, then I would strongly suggest you choose a different term besides "gay Christian."

This isn't just about semantics; the way you identify yourself can affect your spiritual growth. What you believe and how you present yourself to others is what you will continue to walk in. Know that there are other ways to communicate your struggle to those around you without compromising the truth.

Are the Laws of the Old Testament Obsolete?

As I explained, many people are mixing their faith with a fallen sexual identity in hopes of reconciling the two. While I firmly believe that this cannot be done, gay theology has brought forth many carefully crafted arguments for why Christianity and homosexuality are compatible. I would like to address some of the arguments that I feel are becoming increasingly common.

Proponents of gay theology most commonly state that an Old Testament law forbids homosexuality, and that to obey this law without obeying all Old Testament laws is hypocritical. They feel that this is applying one law to others without applying the more inconvenient ones to yourself. This idea is misinformed, and again, proponents of this are often approaching the scriptures with a skewed perception and an intent to justify preconceived ideas.

God gave the Israelites certain rules and laws to instruct them in morality, but also to differentiate them from other nations. The latter laws included how to prepare foods, when to have feasts to honor God, what clothes to wear, and so on. These **Ceremonial Laws** applied only to the Israelites. These actions were meant to signify loyalty to the one and only God, distinguishing the Israelites from the nations that were serving other gods.

The **Moral Laws**, however, were given to all ethnicities. These laws were God's way of telling *all of humanity* that their morality had failed them—that He was the only God they were to serve, the only God who would care and provide for them. These moral laws consisted of universal principles like we see in the Ten Commandments: do not murder, do not serve other gods, to not commit adultery, and so on.

In the Old Testament, all sexual immorality is described as idol worship—as a form of praising another god. All throughout the Bible, we read of nations who served pagan gods and participated in all sorts of sexual deviance. The Philistines and Canaanites in the Old Testament worshiped a giant penis statue! (What guy volunteered to pose for *that* piece? Do you think he got paid well?)

These nations and tribes worshiped the creation instead of the creator; they worshiped their human abilities and bodies, which is what we see in many areas of sexual brokenness, whether it's pornography or masturbation or homosexuality. Instead of the beauty of creation drawing people closer to the One who created it, they're worshiping the creation instead.

The Moral Laws are easier to identify when you realize that they all reflect God's original design for creation (see Rom. 1). Since God clearly states that any sexual activity outside of marriage between a man and a woman is sin and does not represent His will for us, homosexuality violates His design. Therefore, it goes against His moral structure. God never changes.

Jesus says in Mark 10:7, *"It's for this reason that a man leaves his birth family to unite with a woman."* When Jesus came, He fulfilled the law, and now we can honor those laws by being in relationship with Him. We no longer need to follow Ceremonial Laws in order to stay separated from false gods, because we now have the one and only God dwelling in us.

Even though the old laws are fulfilled, and we now live under grace, we must still uphold the Moral Laws if we want to maintain our relationship with Jesus. The New Testament still commands that we walk within God's original design for our own marriages, because restoring humanity's place in the Garden is still in His heart. Morality is now fulfilled by submitting our hearts to God rather than through outward sacrifices, and sex still matters greatly to Him in this New Covenant.

Homosexuality in the New Testament

Another argument you'll hear supporting gay theology is that Jesus never mentions homosexuality or speaks negatively of it. First, I would like to say that there are scriptures addressing homosexuality throughout the New Testament, even if none of them were spoken by Jesus himself. Passages such as Romans 1:26-27, First Corinthians 6:9-10, and First Timothy 1:9-10 tell us how homosexuality is not blessed by God, and these scriptures were given to all cultures and people groups. The idea that they were only intended for one specific culture, like the Ceremonial Laws, is false. This was broad guidance given in the context of an eternal view that spans all cultures and times. From start to finish, the Bible only blesses marriage between a man and a woman.

But still, why *didn't* Jesus say anything about homosexuality? If He's our example of how God loves, then why did He fail to mention something so controversial and important? Well, most of the time, He spoke to a Jewish community that upheld the law. They already had an understanding of what the Word said about all sexual activity outside of a monogamous male/female covenant of marriage, and as such He didn't need to address it. In fact, there were *many* topics He didn't cover during His time on the Earth because they were already understood by His people.

But What About Women in Ministry?

Supporters of gay theology also very commonly use First Timothy 2 to weaken the validity of scripture. This passage appears to suggest that women shouldn't be involved in ministry. Obviously, there are lots of women currently in ministry, so some will point at them and suggest that supporting this practice is hypocritical. If you're okay with ladies leading churches, but you're not okay with homosexuality, aren't you just picking and choosing from the Bible? Once again we see that this is an error when we take a closer look.

In like manner also, that the women adorn themselves in modest apparel, with propriety and moderation, not with braided hair or gold or pearls or costly clothing, but, which is proper for women professing godliness, with good works. Let a woman learn in silence with all submission. And I do not permit a woman to teach or to have authority over a man, but to be in silence. For Adam was formed first, then Eve. And Adam was not deceived, but the woman being deceived, fell into transgression. Nevertheless, she will be saved in childbearing if they continue in faith, love, and holiness, with self-control. (1 Timothy 2:9-15 (NKJV)

Woof. That's pretty heavy right there. When taken alone, it appears to be a pretty damning piece of evidence. However, we begin to understand why Paul said what he said in First Timothy when we look at the context, just as we did with homosexuality and the Leviticus Laws.

Here Paul was addressing a specific church containing a group of women who were former pagan worshipers. The hairstyle Paul refers to was a style that the Ephesian women wore in order to show their allegiance and reverence to the goddess Artemis, a deity from Greek Mythology. Paul encouraged these women to show their reverence and worship to God through loving works, not through a hairstyle.

They were also trained to chant and sing mantras, telling the stories of the Greek gods in order to attract people to the Temple of Artemis. One theologian describes the temple as the "Disneyland" of the time. These women went around calling everyone to stop by, so they could fill them in on the story of Artemis and how she was the mother of all life. According to the story, Artemis helped her mother Leto birth her twin brother Apollo. She then became the goddess of childbearing, and it was believed that if you didn't stay loyal to her you would be cursed in childbirth.

Their belief was that sin entered the world through man, not woman, contradicting what we know from Genesis. So, when Paul said in verse 12, "And I do not permit a woman to teach or to have authority *over* a man, but to be in silence," a truer translation would be that woman is not the author of man, as was the pagan ideology of the day. He was addressing their desire to promote women over men. That's why he then says in verse 13, "For Adam was formed first, then Eve." He wasn't talking about authority here; he was clearing up the true creation story.

When Paul told these women with pagan backgrounds to be silent, he was telling them to stop going around shouting at people about goddesses. He was giving them instructions to keep them in order and away from their old ways. He also reassured them that they would not die in childbirth by not believing in Artemis, and that they were actually saved through the birth of a man (Jesus), which was contrary to what they had been believing.

Finally, Paul mentions women in leadership in other passages and, therefore, we can reason that this particular passage needs to be read in context. The principles remain to this day, but the specific details are not standard. We can have fancy hairstyles, we can wear jewelry, and we can—without a doubt—take part in church leadership.

Prayer

Doctrinal differences exist and will continue to be argued. However, the morality of homosexuality is not a matter of biblical interpretation, as some would claim. This heated debate is currently splitting churches and causing much persecution in the community today because those with influence who do not serve the Lord are pushing for a worldview that is not godly or biblically sound. These ideas and morals are being accepted as truth on a broad scale, and it's causing a lot of damage. Some people claim to serve Christ with their whole heart but twist scriptures so they don't have to surrender their sexuality to God or feel like they're rejecting homosexuals.

My goal isn't to debate anyone here. Jesus doesn't need me to argue for Him. It is important, however, to make sure that we aren't swept up in trends that take us away from God's truth. Truth is what I'm seeking here, and it's what I want to convey.

If you desire to step away from ideologies that you now see are false, I invite you to pray this with me:

Jesus, you are the Word. Your very existence is truth. Please reveal to me, by the help of the Holy Spirit, where I have let my own ideas or pride lead me to beliefs about scripture that were in error. Lord, please reveal to me areas of my life where I am holding onto unhealthy beliefs because I am afraid there is no other way to live and be fulfilled. Help me to remember times when others have pointed out these beliefs as wrong and tried to help me. Please forgive my hard-heartedness and help me discover all you have for me in these areas. Your Word promises that the Holy Spirit will teach us. We are not left alone to figure things out as orphans. We are daughters and you love us and care about us deeply in every way. Thank you for offering us clarity at an even greater level. I receive your forgiveness and guidance. Amen!

Chapter Nine

SSA Liberation

For freedom Christ has set us free; stand firm therefore, and do not submit again to a yoke of slavery.

(Galatians 5:1 ESV)

Let's Talk About Attraction

*S*ometimes what we label as same-sex attraction *is* actually misinterpreted relational needs that we have sexualized in order to fulfill them. So, what is attraction, really? I think there's a lot of confusion surrounding the word as our church communities seek to explain doctrinal truths on the matter.

We have a healthy and God-given tendency to notice and be *drawn to* a person because of their abilities, looks, people skills, gift of leadership, special talents, etc. We are meant to be a light to each other and to reflect God's image. It's a simple fact that you will be attracted to—in other words drawn to—lots of different people in your life. I know I certainly have, and as I unpacked my same-sex attractions with the Lord He gave me an understanding of what this means.

Being attracted to the same sex is not a sin. It's what you do with these attractions that can bring either health or toxicity into your life. When you seek relational and emotional health, you develop a clearer awareness of how the Lord created you and how you should relate to others, but when you twist and contort your attractions you feed into an identity that God did not give you.

When I find myself "attracted" to a woman, I'm still perfectly within God's boundaries. I can think, "Wow, she's beautiful, and she has so many qualities that I admire. I would love to get to know her more." I can celebrate what God has done in her life and ask the Holy Spirit if there are similar areas of my life where I can grow. This attraction is fine because I'm not *eroticizing* it.

This was a huge revelation for me, and one major key to getting free. My self-worth was so low and distorted that I had been eroticizing women that had qualities I felt I was lacking. Because I sensed this strength within them, I thought that they would offer the intimacy I needed. More than anything, I wanted to be loved and to find feminine strength, and this sexualization of my needs was my way of working toward those desires. In my confusion, I worshiped the creation instead of the Creator. Other women became my idol.

My initial attraction was healthy, but I took it to an unhealthy place, indulging in thoughts and actions that were lustful. This provided me with a false sense of satisfaction, which naturally led to obsession. Soon the whole thing became an unfulfilling, self-sabotaging cycle where I never felt satisfied; I was always left needing more, forever running after something I could never obtain. I was continually frustrated and disappointed in my relationships. And even after I returned to the Lord and began to discipline my mind with the help of the Holy Spirit, these learned patterns of obsession and dependency took time to change.

Unlearning relational patterns is a huge part of God restoring health and peace to your life. Now that my mind is renewed, and I understand the power of imagination, I'm no longer greatly tempted to conjure up erotic images of people I'm attracted to. I know that I have authority over sin and that I don't have to partner with it to gain power in my life. Temptation can still arise during difficult times, but the draw of homosexuality is much weaker when I compare it to the relationship I now have with Jesus. He's invested so much in my life, and I truly want to honor Him with all that I am.

It's very easy to become obsessive or compulsive if we lack security in our identity in Christ. If we don't dwell on His truths about us, it leaves room for our natural heart needs to become polluted and twisted. This is an area where even people who don't struggle with same-sex attraction have to submit to the Lord as well, as I have discussed throughout the rest of this book. It's an issue of both disciplining the mind and surrendering one's heart to the Lord. It's a universal concept that applies to every believer, regardless of who they find attractive.

Now if I'm ever attracted to someone and a sexual thought flutters by, I know how to handle it. I reject it. I know that an eroticized thought about another person doesn't come from my New Creation identity. I am crucified with Christ, and according to the Word the things that once had their hooks in me are dead. I have been liberated to enjoy the person God says I am and to express that enjoyment with my husband. Since submitting to God and His discipline, the cheap and easy thrills of lusting after women have lost their appeal. I'm happy to let go of the thought processes that I thought were fulfilling me or keeping me safe from rejection.

As with *any* bondage, it's important to remember that no matter how secure in my true identity I've become, I could always return to old, unhealthy patterns if I chose to fall back on the old lies. I'll say it again: *Everlasting freedom is a moment-by-moment commitment.* Freedom forever requires complete dependence on the Lord. But as much as I rely on Him for every moment of freedom I have, it's not a struggle; I can rest in what He has done for me. The more I've grown in Him and let go of old patterns that I thought defined me, the more Technicolor, power-packed, and wild this ride has become. Religion is not Jesus, ladies. Behavior without the revelation of love is not Jesus. *Boring* is not Jesus.

I now *truly* know His love, and I want to live out that love. This is what sets me free.

Same-Sex Attraction Is Not a Curse

I've known committed Christians who state with no uncertainty that they are just not attracted to the opposite sex. They treat their same-sex attraction like it's simply their burden, their cross to bear. Without having a deeper conversation with them about their own definition of attraction, however, I wouldn't be so quick to identify this as some sort of life sentence. In the same way that God will never use sickness in order to "sanctify" you with a life of longsuffering, sexual attractions that fall outside of His intent are not something He created you with so that you could be some kind of sexual martyr. This is not your "cross to bear."

I see this mindset in some church circles, where people take their lack of opposite-sex attraction as a God-given burden and base their identity on that idea. If this is you, then let me say this: If you desire to be married, and you're free from engaging in homosexual behaviors (including masturbating to images or thoughts of the same sex), then you can trust that this is a healthy desire worth pursuing.

Let's not base our definition of romance and courtship on the world's point of view. Let's not reduce the idea of attraction down to uncontrollable, animalistic tendencies. If you've built a solid friendship with a man who's following the Lord and cares about you, but you don't yet feel the urge to rip his clothes off, that's okay.

It's possible that you're building what some circles might call a "healthy friendship," and passion may come later. Believe me when

I say I've met plenty of people who were not originally attracted sexually to the people that became their spouses, and this includes both same-sex-attracted and opposite-sex-attracted people. Sexual and romantic attraction isn't all or nothing, and it's not completely involuntary and automatic; friendship can lead to intimacy, and intimacy can lead to attraction that wasn't there before. Too many people adhere to the idea of not being attracted to the opposite sex, and they close themselves off to experiencing those attractions by never taking the risk to grow in intimacy with someone of the opposite sex.

All this to say, I urge you never to put limits on God. Please, don't place markers on your life that didn't originate from Him. You are not cursed with same-sex attraction. He took care of all sin on the Cross. There isn't some special sect of people who can't have the complete restoration that God promises the world. Some well-meaning Christians propagate this idea in order to ease the tension in the community, but don't buy into the hype. You may desire to get married, or you may feel called to a life of celibate ministry. Just know that even a celibate person can and should break free from eroticized same-sex attraction. Whatever the case, you can feel secure in knowing that your attractions will align with God's truth as you walk with the Lord and trust Him.

You can have as much liberty as you want if you stay at His table and keep eating the food He prepares for you. *But if you get up and begin feasting on other things at other tables, your old appetites and longings can and will return.* Pride will tell you to leave a bad review Online and go somewhere else when the meal isn't what you expected, or if the service is a little too slow. But just continue to eat and practice thankfulness.

Relationship with God is by no means transactional. Even if we wish we could leave a hefty tip, we can never truly repay what He's done for us. When we abide in Him, seeing our relationship growing and flourishing is all the payment He needs.

It's Time to Be Foolish

There are Christians whose lives are transformed—who are no longer in homosexual relationships and don't experience same-sex attraction in any way. There are Christians who are currently walking out their faith and face temptation at different levels. Some are led by God to marry and some to remain single. All these people walk with God in different ways, but they all give themselves up and accept His transforming love for them. This seems foolish to the world, because the gospel is foolishness.

For the message of the Cross is foolishness to those who are perishing, but to us who are being saved it is the power of God. (1 Corinthians 1:18 NIV)

Surrendering everything that you think is going to bring you peace, happiness, and joy to an invisible God really is something the secular world considers to be *foolish*. This is where the gospel begins: at the cross. We need a life dependent on a loving God who requires everything of us, not so He can withhold, but so He can liberate.

There are many patterns, thought processes, feelings, emotions, and beliefs that seem true as day to our earthly selves, yet scripture teaches us that everything in our hearts falls under God's rule. That means every passion, obsession, desire, and need has to pass through His hands, regardless of our own perception of them.

It's easy to understand why non-believers think the church is hypocritical. This issue of sexuality is extremely messy, and what we don't often like to address is how many people fall into traps of sin because they use ministry as a mask to hide their brokenness. When leaders get caught with their pants down, people watching from the outside point at them and claim that the church is corrupt and that freedom must truly be impossible.

172

And to that, I say Christian failure in the area of sexuality is a *tale as old as time, a song as old as rhyme*. Crack open that dusty old Bible and see for yourself. It's just about stuffed to the brim with faith-filled believers that fell from some pretty high places because of their sex drives. These accounts fill us in on what we still *need* to hear today: we need a savior. We need Jesus. Even Christian leaders need to be asked hard questions in order to keep them accountable just like everyone else.

It takes a personal, loving encounter with Him to leave the path of rejection and despair. No matter what leader falls or whatever ministry topples over for whatever reason, you will still stand as an individual before God at the end of your life. God brings others into your life to offer help, but ultimately, He is the author and finisher of your faith. And if you give yourself permission to sin because you're hurt by the failure of another person or other people, you're really missing out on what Jesus—the Tree of Life—has to offer. He surpasses every failure. He restores all.

Embracing Your Femininity

So far we've covered a lot of general information in this chapter, but now I would like to offer some more practical advice for walking out your freedom. A very big step is embracing your femininity, which includes multiple components.

Let me say this first: **Women, you were made to be sensitive.** I know this is a touchy subject for many women in our current culture, especially those who deal with same-sex attraction. For a long time I avoided all things feminine because I believed that sensitivity equaled weakness. I felt that there was no strength or empowerment in feminine sensitivity. Being sensitive, to me, meant that you were a pushover, a victim, weak. I came to these conclusions after falsely identifying my mother and other sensitive women in my life as weak.

Mom was abused many times when she was younger, and there was no way I was going to allow a man to do the same to me. So, I adjusted my nature in order to keep myself safe and empowered.

I had no idea how wrong I was. I didn't recognize how dull and calloused I was making myself or how I was missing a huge opportunity to engage the Holy Spirit by trying to deny and manipulate my own feminine nature. When we look at examples of sensitivity in the Bible, we don't see weakness or emotionalism; we see discernment and responsiveness. Sensitivity is the ability to reject what is evil and receive what is good. Feminine sensitivity responds and delivers on both a spiritual and emotional level. Even our genitals were created to be sensitive and respond to different stimuli, and our sexuality wouldn't exist without that sensitivity.

As I began to embrace my femininity once more, I gained a stronger understanding of the authority I carried, and the word took on a whole new meaning. I now see my sensitivity as a marker for my spiritual health. Am I growing numb due to life's difficulties and starting to stray toward independence instead of dependence on God? Am I growing overwhelmed because I've observed others not living in freedom and taken on some of their issues?

Or am I perhaps disconnecting from my feminine sensitivity because I've forgotten that God desires His presence to be known and recognized? When I depend on my own strength alone, and wall off my heart because I misunderstand it, I fail to give Him the glory He deserves. But when I walk in sensitivity, I can destroy the enemy's plans and point others to God's presence.

There is nothing more powerful than to walk into a chaotic environment and recognize what God wants to do because you are sensitive to His Holy Spirit. When I sense, I can respond, and when I respond, I can bring change. It's not a posture of being manipulated by Him but of submitting and receiving from Him. And of course, sensitivity manifests differently in different women. We all come from different families and cultures and have a very diverse range of personalities. When you're in a room full of women who are all walking in their true godly identities, it can look and feel much like a vibrant tapestry. We all display our feminine sensitivity in different ways, and the fun is discovering exactly how each of us carries this nature of God in our lives.

Lipstick and Dresses

Another aspect of my femininity that God restored and defined was how I presented myself visually to the world. When I was sexually involved with women and fantasizing about them, I was repulsed by the idea of dressing in anything soft, putting on makeup, or even having my hair long. I was looking for feminine *strength*, after all, and all that foofy girly stuff felt like another sign of weakness.

Now, I'm not saying you can't totally rock your femininity in pants, no makeup, and a pixie cut. There are plenty of straight girls who just aren't into dressing pretty and there are ones who identify as lesbians who are all about it. I'm simply showing you my thought process during this time. Expression can vary from person to person, though I do think certain heart issues can be universal.

For me, throwing away my makeup and chopping off my long hair was about denying and manipulating my femininity. During this time of my life, I wanted to strip away all the girlish "cues," I had observed growing up. I rejected my upbringing and the God-fearing tribe I had come from. I wasn't going to be a tea party Bible study women's group member who sat at a kitchen table with the other church ladies and laughed at Joyce Meyer tapes. Nope, I decided to associate with a crew that didn't appear to be weak and vulnerable.

The ideal image I was shooting for was *unbreakable*. I idolized brash individualism. Step on those flowers with your big army boots, Liz! Squash their pretty, petaly little heads! No one can touch you now! But of course, as we've seen all too much in this book, my search for authority over the darkness that tormented me only perpetuated my pain. The desire to destroy that pain was from God, but how I went about it was not in His plan.

One problem was that even before I began pursuing my same-sex attractions, I wasn't exactly set up for success in this department. I'm a creative person. I love art and color. However, growing up out in the boondocks with a super low self-esteem and almost no money for anything other than the absolute basics, nice clothes and makeup weren't in great supply in our home.

My mother loved to paint her nails and go shopping when the budget allowed it, but my overweight self had very few choices. Since I hated my body, I ultimately gravitated toward what was comfy and didn't attract too much attention. This allowed me to transition quite comfortably into full-on femininity-shunning mode when I hit my senior year.

After I returned to the Lord and began to understand my femininity, I began to see a natural progression. I found myself wanting to relate with other Christian women in terms of how I presented myself. Honestly, I think much of this came from a desire to belong. Don't get me wrong, I had friends who loved me however I dressed and whether or not I put on makeup in the morning. I'm not saying that I had to look like everyone else in order to fit in. These aspects of our appearance are ultimately trivial things that don't define us; by no means are they deep heart matters. However, our appearance does give cues to those around us that either say "keep out" or "welcome." For that reason, it's good to pay attention to what signals we might be sending to those around us.

Through managing my appearance, God awakened a desire within me to be expressive and embrace my love of color. I began to better care for my body. Since women were now friends and sisters in the Lord, rather than idols I used for self-fulfillment, I could receive inspiration from them about expressing my femininity. Things I once deemed worthless—like makeup, clothes, and earrings—were commonalities I wanted to share. This stuff was still trivial in the grand scheme of things, but nevertheless it was a valuable *shared experience.*

As I awakened to this part of me, I had a strong, God-given desire to join others and to fit into a community where I knew I belonged. Sure, this was difficult at times, seeing as I had always prided myself on my independence. But the more I allowed my heart to be free from my own preconceived ideas of what a woman should be in order to protect that independence, the more I found myself wanting to buy lipstick and dresses. Uncomfortable shoes, well...I'm still working on that one. But lipstick and dresses? Absolutely. I went out and learned more about makeup and other things usually seen as *girlie.* This new form of expression did a lot to pull me naturally into a community of women. Some women love big, bold colors and others like a more natural look, so it was fun swapping tips and discovering what kinds of styles I liked myself.

Makeup didn't make me feminine, but allowing myself to be expressive and embracing the qualities God gave me did. Through all of this, I began to soften and welcome friendships in new and healthy ways. When I got married, I had fun learning what aspects of my appearance my husband responded to. Andy is a fun, warm British man, and he's never put any pressure on me to look a certain way. Over time I have noticed, however, that whenever I put on a lot of makeup and put extra effort into dressing up, he responds strongly. I learned that he *loves* when I doll myself up, and I often tease him about it. You know those old glamour shots from the 90's? Yeah. That. The bigger the hair and makeup, the more he lights up.

So, of course, I try to strike a balance; my inner hippie loves to go braless and wear pants with elastic bands, but when I want to send him an extra little message that I care, I cake on the makeup. He'll still hit on me when I look my absolute worst, but he very much feels the love when I break out the mascara.

How you allow the Lord to bring out your femininity will differ depending on who you are and what role He has for you. Do you absolutely need to dress a certain way? No. We are made in both the feminine and masculine image of God, and no one can pigeonhole you into adopting a certain look. In fact, I know plenty of missionaries who have been called as single women into countries ruled by misogynistic men, and they would be terrorized (and their godly work hindered) if they wore hair extensions and high heels.

There are aspects of traditional feminine expression that I am still not rockin' at. You may shine in ways that I don't and vice versa. That's perfectly okay. That's the adventure in all this. You get to explore your femininity with an open heart. Discovery with Him is what matters.

Just remember that we do have vaginas, and as such, there are likely certain qualities that we were made to reflect. Be open to the idea that you may find yourself reflecting one of God's feminine characteristics that you hadn't considered. Whatever the case, however your clothes, hair, or makeup look, you go out and rock that femininity. Discover and embrace how the Lord created you.

Experiencing Rejection from Other Christians

The last thing I want to talk about regarding how the Lord brought clarity and healing to my feminine nature is *affection*. By affection, I don't just mean hugs and whatnot, but also friendship and quality time.

It's funny (not really funny, but you know what I mean) that I was once so starving for affection in my life, yet it left me feeling so empty when I sought after it in an illegitimate way. Naturally, learning how to seek it out the right way was sometimes difficult. Anyone who has chosen to address their unhealthy same-sex attraction can probably relate to being cautious of expressing or receiving affection from members of the same sex when first learning to walk out their wholeness. You're relearning where the boundaries are and allowing the Lord to restructure your understanding of friendships. You are moving away from the codependent model of living life. There is awkwardness, but also a strong desire to be loved. You may sometimes find yourself outside of the boundaries, with the Lord gently nudging you back. During this process, it's too easy to go on something of an affection lockdown because you're scared of how people might perceive you. There can be a lot of tension, especially when people in the church hear your story.

One incident in my mid-twenties still stands out to me. Like 99.98% of the women in my church, I was swept up by scrapbooking mania for a short time. (It might have gone on longer, but you can only fill so many books with pictures of your cats before you have to really stop and look at your life.) One day a friend and I went to an acquaintance's house to do some scrapbooking. This girl was about the same age as us and didn't know much about me, but she was very fun and welcoming. We shared our testimonies as we worked, and eventually I shared about my struggle with homosexuality.

Our host instantly stiffened up as though I had just confessed to a murder. She didn't say anything about it, but it was obvious that there was now a distance between us. When we left, I didn't hug her goodbye, and I didn't make any attempts to be affectionate with her after that. In fact, her reaction had such an effect on me that I decided not to share my story with many people going forward for fear that they would reject me as well. I felt renewed shame, and that caused me to guard myself.

I've come a long way since then. Now I know that people who respond to vulnerability defensively or with rejection often are struggling with their own insecurities. When image is super important to you, you'll attempt to keep things looking perfect even at the cost of those around you. I've forgiven that girl and moved on, but I've had time to look back and realize how I guarded myself because of what I felt was a shameful moment.

The Lord has beautifully restored my ability to be vulnerable and to show affection with women in my community. This acquaintance wasn't the only person who found it difficult to be open or affectionate with me when she learned about my past experiences, and she might not even be the last. But now I share my testimony without reservation whenever I feel led to do so, and I have more friends than I can count that have welcomed me with open arms.

Affection with Women

As of writing this book, my husband and I have lived in the Charlotte, North Carolina area for almost five years. Moving from the West to the East Coast was a culture shock, to say the least. I had been a card-carrying California girl my whole life, so naturally much about this place surprised me. One very beautiful and surprising thing was how welcoming and loving the women in my church were. Not all of my friends are originally from here, yet there is an incredible grace on this area for women to express their affections like I've never seen before.

When I first arrived, I was running a small business, focused on my vision of *funding* ministries—not *starting* one. Things didn't go exactly according to plan though and sometime near the beginning of 2014 I found myself alone in my living room, talking with the Lord. My investor had backed out, I had no job, my husband was using our car to commute three hours a day, and we couldn't afford a second one. My idea of how things *should* have turned out looked nothing like reality. Feeling stripped of everything, I asked the Lord what He would like me to do.

Very clearly, He spoke to my heart, "I have hedged you in. It's time to write."

And with that, I knew that I was being called into ministry to tell my story, so others would be set free. This led to another "coming out," as it were; I began a blog series about my testimony and it became public knowledge. At that time, we had just transitioned to a new church, and I began writing my first book only a few weeks after our first Sunday.

I was very much aware that I was in the South—the Bible Belt, no less—speaking publicly about sexual issues that church people usually like to avoid. We had just found a new home and a new church, and I knew that the risk of rejection was great. What if it tore down what we had only just started to build? That didn't matter though; I felt a boldness I had never experienced before. This wasn't about me, this was about Him. This was about giving my good Father the credit and glory He deserved so that others would better know Him.

The blog was one thing, but when I finally published *The God of My Parents* and handed copies out to my friends and leadership, I braced for impact. I imagined what it would be like to walk into church that Sunday: the stares, the awkward silence, the squirming discomfort when I sat down next to someone… But to my surprise, it was nothing like that. Not only was my community just as welcoming as ever, but they gave their full support for who I was and what God had done in my life. My friends became even more affectionate toward me and absolutely covered me in love.

Can I hear you say "BREAKTHROUGH!" Where I expected things to be costly, the Lord met me with a gift. I have learned so much from these ladies over the last few years. They're a diverse group, too: homeschool moms, single women, women in ministry, business women, the list goes on. They have this way of carrying each other's burdens in very practical ways, and they challenge me to grow in my femininity whenever I'm with them. Whenever they sense that I'm in pain, they don't allow me to isolate myself. They're also not afraid of physical affection, and they have this acute ability to affirm parts of my femininity that I didn't even know I needed more strength in. In fact, my friend Jaynie is like some sort of hybrid shopper superhero, and my tastes in fashion have dramatically changed just since I started hanging out with her. Why am I buying floral blouses? How did this happen? Oh yeah, *What Would Jaynie Do?*

These ladies have taught me the value of the thank you card. Dear Lord, I never realized the power these things held. They've also taught me the value of a cooked meal brought over during hard times. They've continually prayed and believed with me and Andy as we've struggled with infertility. They're not afraid to love someone who has mishandled friendships in the past. They love so well that some of the simplest acts of feminine expression have become the most impactful. I never want to forget this season in my life, and I will hold onto these lessons they've taught me forever.

Even before moving to the East Coast, God blessed me with many amazing friends throughout my journey. Some of these helped me find pieces of myself that I had shoved into a box somewhere in order to protect myself. Some of them had the difficult task of working with me when I was fresh outta' Egypt.

My dear friend Denise is a hair stylist and has worked with me for over fifteen years, gently pushing me to explore new parts of my femininity. Time in her salon has become something of a sacred ritual. I'll show up with her iced, nonfat latte with whipped cream (you don't want to know what happens if you show up in the morning without her iced, nonfat latte with whipped cream). Then I'll sit in her chair and she'll suggest new styles and colors, all while asking me about how things are going in my life. Early on in my journey, I couldn't afford to pay her much, so she only charged me half price, and the resulting compliments I got on my hair brought an extra layer of healing to my life that I simply wouldn't have had access to without her. From the start, she brought me in as her younger sister and made sure I was cared for.

I had many women like this in my life. My spiritual mother is a woman named Harriet, and throughout my life she has provided a continual example of strong, authentic femininity. She's known me since I was ten years old and was there through all of our family's troubles and all of my own poor life choices. She was there during my formative years to model sensitivity to the Holy Spirit, and she was there to call me back to my identity when I had fallen away.

I will never forget all the hours she spent with me as I struggled to give my life back over to the Lord in my college years. Once, before I had fully disclosed to her that I was returning to the faith, we were sitting in a cafe together. At one point she looked at me and said, "I feel like you're beginning to soften." At the time I resented her words, but now I treasure the memory of that moment. It marked a turning point in my life and was evidence of the transformative power of Jesus.

Your walk may look different from mine, and you may experience rejection from some members of the church. It may take time to find women who are willing to pour into you. But if you open yourself up, you can trust that God will bring people into your life to help you through this process. Affection with other women may be a little uncomfortable now, but He will make sure your needs are met.

Prayer

This is by no means an exhaustive account of how the Lord has continually addressed my same-sex attraction and restored my femininity. I just wanted to give you a glimpse of what He's done in hopes of stirring up your faith and encouraging you to ask the Lord to grow your identity. We all need to be free to express how He made us. We all need Jesus to restore identity in our lives.

If you struggle with same-sex attraction or you have stripped away your femininity in order to protect yourself and would like the Lord to visit you in these areas, I invite you to say this prayer. Some of you may have never struggled with same-sex attraction but still have problems expressing your femininity, and if this is the case I invite you to pray as well.

Jesus, thank you for knowing me more than I know myself. Whatever stage of development I'm in, I know that your desire is for ALL of me to be loved. Help me to see where I have stripped away or hidden my femininity in order to pursue strength on my own terms. Break the chains that hinder me from entering into healthy relationships with other women, so that I can find my place in the community. Forgive me for taking this into my own hands. Help me discern where I can better trust you and where I can grow my feminine expression in new ways. Thank you for caring about the things I care about. Thank you for liberating me in every way. Amen!

Chapter Ten

Jesus, the Rule Breaker

"Every single human being is created in the image of God; created for dignity, created for the Father's love, created for kindness, created for mercy."

—Heidi Baker

From Genesis to Revelation, God's pursuit of your heart is evident. There is no obstacle created by you or others that can keep you from the love of God. Throughout the gospel, Jesus broke all the religious rules in order to liberate women. These women were often marked by society as outcasts and oppressed by racism, sexism, and poverty, and yet they were touched by His pursuit of them in the midst of their pain. Jesus liberated them from oppression and sin when everyone else wanted to judge and condemn them.

Some of these women didn't choose the circumstances that bound them. Others probably didn't see any other choice than to give away their sexual dignity in exchange for some sort of security.

As much as the religious people of Jesus' day mocked and ridiculed Him for it, a huge part of Jesus' mission was to set women free. He didn't care about how the public saw Him; in every instance He loved these women openly, healed their broken hearts, and equipped them.

Jesus Anointed by a Sinful Woman

One of the Pharisees asked him to eat with him, and he went into the Pharisee's house and reclined at table. And behold, a woman of the city, who was a sinner, when she learned that he was reclining at table in the Pharisee's house, brought an alabaster flask of ointment, and standing behind him at his feet, weeping, she began to wet his feet with her tears and wiped them with the hair of her head and kissed his feet and anointed them with the ointment.

Now when the Pharisee who had invited him saw this, he said to himself, "If this man were a prophet, he would have known who and what sort of woman this is who is touching him, for she is a sinner." (Luke 7:36-39 ESV)

This is one of the greatest examples of Jesus' rule-breaking passion and of His desire to release women from the things that bind them. Jesus interrupted Simon's mockery with the parable of the two debtors, which is one we can all get behind for many reasons. One man owed a ton of money and one owed a little. When neither could pay, the moneylender canceled both their debts.

Jesus then asked Simon who would love the moneylender more. Simon gave a smart-alecky reply: the one who owed more. I can easily picture Simon scoffing at Jesus' simple parable and wondering what the heck it had to do with a disgraceful and embarrassing public display of affection from a prostitute.

Therefore I tell you, her sins, which are many, are forgiven —for she loved much. But he who is forgiven little, loves little." And he said to her, "Your sins are forgiven." Then those who were at table with him began to say among themselves, "Who is this, who even forgives sins?" And he said to the woman, "Your faith has saved you; go in peace." (Luke 7:47-50 ESV)

This is one of my favorite scriptures. It's more than likely that the Pharisees invited Jesus to dinner to find fault in his teachings. Then a woman walked into their religious mess, and her sins were so many that she was only identified as "one who is immoral." This woman loved much. The fact that she braved such a harsh religious culture to encounter Jesus is astounding to me. She began to weep in her conviction of sin and in adoration of her all-embracing Savior.

In modern terms, this is akin to Lord and Lady Grantham inviting Jesus to Downtown Abbey for a cup of a tea only to have a porn star bust in and start kissing His feet. In that setting, Jesus would have every right to put up a strong boundary against such an intimate encounter with a woman. But Jesus the Christ brought conviction to the immoral woman by loving her instead of having her thrown out. Too many people believe that this kind of person deserves nothing more than to be shunned, but this woman had likely been shunned her entire life. His goodness freed her from her false identity and led her to accept the one He had given her.

Simon, of course, just had to whip out his sin-measuring tool to use on this woman. He snidely suggested that if Jesus were a true prophet, He would know her sins. First, talk about a rude host! Second, this was an open invitation for Jesus to school him with one of those perfect Jesus-style silent rebukes. Our great multitasking Savior killed two birds with one stone, bringing forgiveness and healing to a sinful woman, while shutting down a religious Pharisee who saw no need for salvation from his own sin and projected all sorts of nonsense onto other people and their failures.

The word "saved" in the Greek is "sozo," which means "to give new life" and "to cause to have a new heart." When we are saved, we are healed, cured, preserved, kept safe, rescued from danger and destruction, and delivered. We are saved from physical death through healing and from spiritual death through the forgiveness of sin and its effects.

Jesus saved this woman. He saw the injustice of the Pharisee's reaction to her and responded by forgiving her sins and setting her soul free from the things that bound it. But it's so important to see how saving her wasn't simply about giving her the love and acceptance that other people refused her; it was about restoring the identity God had given her and freeing her to **go and sin no more**. Embracing her did *not* mean sleeping with her.

Okay, I know that's a weird thing to say, but hear me out. As we've discussed, too often a person's answer to sin is to simply accept it. When believers see other people who are hurting, sometimes they accept everything about them to prevent further pain. Sometimes they try to answer a person's needs on that person's own terms.

People often come to the conclusion that the way to treat sexual brokenness is with sex, and we see this a lot in the area of homosexuality; what better way to bring a man out of same-sex attraction than to have him sleep with a woman? Or if he can't seem to free himself of same-sex attraction, won't he be better off in a homosexual relationship so at least he's not alone?

The woman in this story was most likely a prostitute as both a means of surviving and as a way to meet her emotional need for intimacy. If Jesus had wanted to answer her need on her own terms, that would have meant sleeping with her, thus giving her what her heart craved. But that's not how Jesus works. Her sin may have come from a legitimate need, but the woman's creator answered that need in His own way. He addressed the perception that was holding her captive and released her to move forward without sin. Jesus declared her whole because of her response to His love—a love that doesn't require reciprocation but is so moving to God when it is reciprocated.

The Woman at the Well

Another wonderful example of Jesus breaking all the religious rules to see a woman set free is the story of the Woman at the Well. This account in John's gospel is very famous, the subject of countless sermons. I've heard a lot of them use the passage to basically say, "No matter your past, even if you're a total harlot, Jesus can still forgive you." While that's true, I feel that there's a richness to the story that's often overlooked.

The road before Jesus and His disciples—from Judea to Galilee—was a precarious one. John 4 begins by describing the escalating tension in the area. The Pharisees weren't too happy with Jesus' workings and they were stirring the pot however they could. Instead of sticking around to argue with them, Jesus jetted off on a mission to accomplish the will of the Father. He knew He had better things to do than defend Himself to deaf ears.

He and his disciples took the route through Samaria. Jews normally went around Samaria, despite the fact that this made the trip much longer. See, the Jews despised the Samaritans. They segregated themselves and set in place many rules and regulations for trading with them. They did everything in their power to make sure the two races never mingled.

The Samaritans were actually descendants of the Israelites; after the fall of Samaria in 722BC, they were the ones who intermarried with the foreigners that conquered it. This resulted in a new and unique culture. The Samaritans only chose to follow the first five books of the Old Testament and mixed in some of the pagan beliefs they took from their interracial and interreligious spouses. Because of this, they became much-hated rivals of the Jews. So naturally, Jesus' decision to cut through Samaria was a pretty big deal.

Despite the directness of this route, it was still going to take Jesus and company two or three days to get where they were going. After traveling for some time, Jesus decided to stop and rest at Jacob's Well, which is a famous well in Sychar. This place offered a lovely view of the Samaritans' temple on Mt. Gerzim. (The Samaritans weren't allowed to worship at the temple in Jerusalem, so they built a competing temple up on the mountain. The proper place to worship was a hot debate between the two people groups at the time.)

The group was tired and hungry, so they went further into town to grab some dinner. Jesus stayed at the well alone. His disciples probably considered it odd that He wanted to stay there without anything to draw up the water. As He rested, a Samaritan woman came to the well to get water for herself, and He began to speak with her.

All Samaritans were excluded and rejected by the Jews, but as we've too often seen throughout history, it was the women who bore the brunt of it all. According to the law, a Jewish woman was "unclean" while she was menstruating and was prohibited from coming into contact with her family during and immediately after her cycle. A Samaritan woman, however, was deemed unclean the moment she was born. All Samaritan women were unclean at all times and were to be avoided. To the Jews, they were about as valuable as dogs, and they were treated as such.

That being said, even the simple act of speaking to this woman broke a laundry list of rules. Even apart from her being a Samaritan, Jesus—a Rabbi—was prohibited from speaking to a woman without her husband being present. As usual, Jesus did not care about these laws and asked her for a drink.

A woman from Samaria came to draw water. Jesus said to her, "Give me a drink." (For his disciples had gone away into the city to buy food.) The Samaritan woman said to him, "How is it that you, a Jew, ask for a drink from me, a woman of Samaria?" (For Jews have no dealings with Samaritans.) Jesus answered her, "If you knew the gift of God, and who it is that is saying to you, 'Give me a drink,' you would have asked him, and he would have given you living water." The woman said to him, "Sir, you have nothing to draw water with, and the well is deep. Where do you get that living water? Are you greater than our father Jacob? He gave us the well and drank from it himself, as did his sons and his livestock." Jesus said to her, "Everyone who drinks of this water will be thirsty again, but whoever drinks of the water that I will give him will never be thirsty again. The water that I will give him will become in him a spring of water welling up to eternal life." The woman said to him, "Sir, give me this water, so that I will not be thirsty or have to come here to draw water." (John 4:7–15 ESV)

My goodness, there is literally nothing about this interaction that fit with the rules. Not only did He talk with her— illegal—but then He asked to drink from the same vessel as her—super illegal—and drew her into a conversation so that He could teach her—extra illegal. Seriously, even teaching a Samaritan woman was against the rules! But Jesus engaged her with a huge purpose. It was an amazing sign of a humble God. Finally, He took things to another level and revealed Himself. He wasn't just a rule-breaking Rabbi or an all-knowing prophet, but the Christ!

Jesus said to her, "Go, call your husband, and come here." The woman answered him, "I have no husband." Jesus said to her, "You are right in saying, 'I have no husband'; for you have had five husbands, and the one you now have is not your husband. What you have said is true." The woman said to him, "Sir, I perceive that you are a prophet. Our fathers worshiped on this mountain, but you say that in Jerusalem is the place where people ought to worship."

Jesus said to her, "Woman, believe me, the hour is coming when neither on this mountain nor in Jerusalem will you worship the Father. You worship what you do not know; we worship what we know, for salvation is from the Jews. But the hour is coming, and is now here, when the true worshipers will worship the Father in spirit and truth, for the Father is seeking such people to worship him. God is spirit, and those who worship him must worship in spirit and truth." The woman said to him, "I know that Messiah is coming (he who is called Christ). When he comes, he will tell us all things." Jesus said to her, "I who speak to you am he." (John 4:16–26 ESV)

Today, there is some debate surrounding this woman. Most people assume that the mention of many husbands means she was yet another harlot, but technically it's also possible that she was simply a Samaritan in need of saving just like all the others. So, which do I think it was? Was she a woman of the night? A sexual deviant? A dirty sinner? I think those things are possible, and there are bigger themes in the story we can take away regardless, but I like to stay open to the possibility that there was more to the story. Simply labeling her as another woman in deep sexual sin can easily cause you to overlook the true depth of the story and conclude only that the passage is about Jesus loving sinners. Plus, there's plenty of evidence to support the opposing theory.

First off, during this time it was very difficult for a woman to get a divorce, let alone five. In order to divorce her husband, he would either have to die or ask for the divorce himself. It's very likely that each of her five marriages ended in death or rejection. It's interesting how Jesus points out that, "...the one you now have is not your husband." Most take this to mean some sort of infidelity, but this isn't necessarily true either. In those days, the Roman government didn't allow former Samaritan slaves to marry whoever they wanted; they could only marry those with Roman-born citizenship. If either the woman or her partner were former slaves, their marriage wouldn't be legally binding.

Since marriage was vital to a woman's security in those days, the pain caused by so many failed marriages probably left her heartbroken. When Jesus mentioned her husbands and her illegitimate relationship, there's no proof that He was doing this to point out her sin. It's very likely that He was simply showing His supernatural knowledge of her and communicating that He knew of her isolation and pain. There's nothing condemning about what He said; He was only trying to draw her in. Jesus often said, "Go and sin no more," to the sinners whose lives He touched. But He didn't say that here.

It's also worth noting that theirs is the longest recorded conversation between Jesus and anyone, and she was the first person to whom He revealed Himself to be the Messiah. Judging by their exchange, it's obvious that this woman's intellect was high. A notoriously loose woman wouldn't be allowed into conversations of politics and such with a man, yet she asked Jesus very pertinent questions about the political and religious circumstances of her day. She truly wanted to know where the best place to worship was.

The scripture goes on to say that after Jesus revealed Himself to be the Messiah, she ran into town and told all the men what had taken place. If this woman were nothing but a floozy, I'm not sure if they would have listened to or believed her. But they did listen, and they invited Jesus into their community where He led many of them to the Lord.

All in all, I would say there's a compelling case for the woman at the well being an intelligent, respected woman. It may seem like an insignificant detail, considering that Jesus was still breaking every rule in the book by talking to her and the overall message is ultimately the same, but I believe it makes the story so much stronger. We can't simply dismiss the woman at the well as one more case of Jesus bringing grace to society's castaways. Such an oversimplification cheapens the story.

Jesus had a deep exchange with this woman, and through that exchange He was able to bring life to an entire community. He very purposely stopped at that well so that He could connect with her. She wasn't an incidental piece in a greater story where He came to save the day; He included her because she had an important part to play in her people's salvation. He cut through all the taboo and religious mess to capture her heart, and from there she spread the good news.

And I don't know about you, but I think that's extraordinary.

Prayer

As we saw with both women in this chapter, the King of the Universe is forever cutting through barriers to get to our hearts. Despite all the things in this world that try to keep you from His truth and push you off His path, He's still in wild pursuit of you. He's willing to meet you in the room full of Pharisees, the place where others have rejected and shamed you. He's willing to receive your adoration and worship when some would tell you it's inappropriate and question your worthiness. He's willing to break every religious rule that tells women with sexual issues that they're too unclean to go before God.

It is a biblical truth that you were meant for liberty in your mind, body, and emotions. Living a life of sexual liberty, whether you're single or married, is about receiving grace and cultivating a heart that is completely open to Him. He doesn't want us to give up sin in our lives for His love; He wants us to give it up because of

His love. His love for us is unending, unchanging, and eternal, but when we truly accept that love and live a life that's completely dependent on Him, our lives become a gift back to Him. We become living reflections of His love. We understand what it means to be daughters of God.

You may feel disqualified from serving a purpose in the kingdom of God because of your past. You may have faced challenges that left you wondering how the Lord sees you. You may have decided that your life has no value, and that you are beyond redeeming. If so, I would like you to pray this with me:

Jesus, I need your truth now more than ever. Please let me see my life from your perspective and see what you can bring about through my surrendered heart. Please break off any religious ideas or false conclusions I might be carrying that limit my purpose and destiny.

I recognize that nothing in my past has disqualified me from your love. I receive a fresh vision for my life and I invite you to come and break all the rules in your quest for my heart. Thank you, Jesus, for your unending love. Thank you for making all things new. Amen!

Chapter Eleven
A Few Final Words

"Gee, what happened to all the French macarons?"

—Liz G. Flaherty

I hope you've enjoyed your time on The Couch. I'm sorry I couldn't offer you my real one to sit on, though it's probably for the best seeing as by now one of the cats might have migrated to your lap and left you with a much larger hair problem.

More than anything, my hope is that you gained a better vision of the Lord's plan for your life, much as I did during the many hours I racked up on various couches over the years. I pray your eyes and your heart were opened to receiving His abundance. I pray that more and more women begin to discover that Adam and Eve may have left the physical Garden behind, but Eden is open to us all. Jesus reopened the gates when He gave His life for our sins, and He's inviting us all to walk with Him again.

And honestly, I would like to thank you. I want to thank each and every woman who took the time to read this book and prayerfully consider her sexuality and how it relates to her walk with the Lord. The most intimate places of your heart, mind, and body are sacred and highly valued by Him. Taking time with the Holy Spirit to be deliberate in addressing these areas of your life requires a great level of bravery. So, thank you for allowing my voice to be one that invites you to find a greater depth of freedom with Jesus. I value and pray for you, and I wholeheartedly believe that great things are in store for each one of you.

If you would like to experience more of the Lord's love and freedom in your life, and you still don't quite know where to start, feel free to close out our time together with this prayer:

Lord, I invite you to break apart my false perceptions of you and reveal the truth of who you really are. I invite you to mess up my skewed ideas of how you see me and reveal that I was created in your perfect image. Holy Spirit, I invite you to lead me to every truth about my identity in Christ, as the Word promises you will do. Help me to understand what it truly is to receive your love and to love you with all of my heart, so that I can walk free from the entanglement of sin and grow in maturity.

Lord, thank you for being the author and finisher of my faith. Thank you for always pursuing me. Thank you for being a wonderful father who loves me. I genuinely ask for your help and guidance, and I know that you are right here with me, ready to lead.

I'm ready.

Take me to Eden.

AMEN!

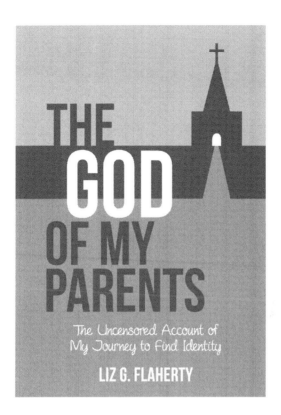

Since a young age Liz has struggled to fit in. Her traditional Christian upbringing is always at odds with her environment; she's self-conscious about her weight; she feels attracted to other women and doesn't know why. When her pain comes to a boiling point she makes a decision – one that marks a radical turning point in her life.

Walk with Liz as she struggles with fear, rejection, grief, substance abuse, her sexuality, and above all things, her faith. Witness the beautiful transformation of one woman in her quest to find both herself and God. Sometimes heartbreaking, often hilarious, and always totally honest, The God of My Parents is a message of hope and a testament to His redemptive power.

www.lizgflaherty.com
Facebook – Liz G Flaherty
Instagram – Liz G Flaherty

24097503R00111

Made in the USA
San Bernardino, CA
02 February 2019